Medals of America
Presents

United States Military Medals 1939 to Present

By
Lawrence H. Borts
and
Col. (Ret.) Frank C. Foster

2nd Edition

*Dedicated To
America's finest citizens;
her veterans and active military
with the families who support them...
God Bless you all !*

Hardcover Edition ISBN - 1-884452-10-8
Softcover Edition ISBN - 1-884452-11-6

Library of Congress
Catalog Card Number - 93-80445

Published by:
MOA Press (Medals of America Press)
1929 Fairview Road, Fountain Inn S. C.
29644-9137
(803) 862-6425

Printed in the United States of America

ABOUT THE AUTHORS

LONNY BORTS

Lawrence "Lonny" Borts developed a lifelong interest in military awards as a boy in New York City during World War II. After graduating from the New York University College of Engineering, he spent most of his professional life with the Grumman Corporation, retiring in 1992 as an Engineering Specialist. He maintains one of the largest collections of military ribbons in the world and is consultant to a number of U. S. Armed Forces directorates and medals research societies. He is also the Awards Program Director of Vanguard, Inc., the largest supplier of military uniform equipment in the U. S. and realized every enthusiast's dream when he co-designed the Coast Guard "E" Ribbon. He and Beverly, his bride of nearly 40 years, now reside in Melbourne, Florida.

FRANK FOSTER

Col. Frank C. Foster (USA , Ret'd), graduated from The Citadel in 1964 and saw service as a Battery Commander in Germany and in Vietnam with the 173rd Airborne Brigade. In the Adjutant General's Corps he served as the Adjutant General of the Central Army Group, the 4th Infantry Division and was the Commandant and Chief of the Army's Adjutant General's Corps from 1986 to 1990. His military service provided him a unique view of the Armed Forces Awards System. He currently operates Medals of America Press. He and his wife Linda, who was decorated with the Army Commander's Medal in 1990, live in Fountain Inn, South Carolina.

GRATEFUL ACKNOWLEDGEMENTS

The authors wish to express their deepest appreciation to the following individuals for their invaluable contributions. Without their unselfish efforts, this book would have ended as an unfilled dream.

Richard Bush for color plates. Mr. Bush makes fine art prints and custom enlarging and studied photography under Jerry Ulesmann at the University of Florida.

The entire Medals of America team including: Mrs. Doris Hegler, Mrs. Lois Owens, Mrs. Linda Foster, Major Bill Foss and Mr. Andy Williams of R. L. Bryan (Printers).

Mr. Gerald T. Luchino, Mr. Thomas B. Proffitt, and Mr. Robert L. Hopkins of The Institute of Heraldry, U.S. Army.

Mr. F. P. Anthony, currently serving as Head of the U. S. Marine Corps Military Awards Branch, Human Resources Division.

Ms. Shelby (Jeanne) Kirk, currently serving as Head of the U. S. Navy Awards and Special Projects Branch.

Ms. Dianne E. Porter, currently serving as Chief, U. S. Coast Guard Medals and Awards Branch.

Master Warrant Officer Rick Nelson, currently serving with the U.S. Army Awards Branch.

MSgt Scott Kilbride, currently serving as Chief of the U. S. Air Force Recognition Programs Branch - Recognition and Special Programs Division.

CMSgt. Steve Haskin, Ribbon Bank Manager of the Orders and Medals Society of America.

Mr. Bill Gershen, President and CEO of Vanguard, Inc.

Ms. Patricia A. Thomas, Office of Maritime Labor & Training, Maritime Administration, Department of Transportation.

LT(jg) Jim Mathieu, U. S. Coast Guard Defense Operations Division.

TABLE OF CONTENTS

LIST OF ILLUSTRATIONS

1. INTRODUCTION

One evening, just as I was about to wrap up my day's activities, I received a telephone call which started off with the words: "Why haven't I heard of you before?". The caller introduced himself as a Mr. Lonny Borts and, when I said I have never heard of **him** either, we both laughed and figured we were probably even. The obvious answer is that our company has always focused on veterans, rather than collectors and researchers, so there was little likelihood that we would cross paths in spite of the same organizations to which we belong .

When Lonny described some of the work he was doing in the decorations and awards field, my level of excitement rose and I asked him to send me a copy of his latest article. After reading his material, it was clear that Lonny Borts is one of the foremost experts in the U.S. Military awards field. His work is so impressive in level of detail and completeness that I immediately proposed a book to cover the entire spectrum of U.S. Military awards since World War II.

The collaborative effort arising from that first exchange of ideas has culminated in this book, a volume which is designed as a definitive reference covering United States decorations, medals and ribbons, including; history, background, authority, attachments, the rules for wear and ideas for mounting.

This book has two main purposes; first to provide veterans and active duty personnel a complete reference since 1939 and second to provide a single source which covers the awards of each branch of the service. I hope we have done this and we look forward to help from our readers to improve the future editions.

Most of the material is derived from the latest military awards and uniform manuals and other authoritative sources, but the authors must confess that personal opinions may have slipped in from time to time.

As long as confessions are in order, some other pitfalls involved in generating such a text should be addressed here. In any effort involving all the U.S. Armed Services, the matter of award names is one of the most vexing to a writer and most obvious to students of the subject. As a prime example, the existence of four Distinguished Service Medals and five Commendation Medals, Achievement Medals and Good Conduct Medals forces the use of the form: "Navy Distinguished Service Medal", "Army Commendation Medal" and "Joint Service Achievement Medal" no matter what is stated in the applicable Awards Manual.

Guaranteeing that any book is absolutely up-to-date is also a potential hazard, especially in the dynamic world of U.S. Awards which has produced an average of 1 1/2 new awards per year since the unification of the Armed Forces in 1947, (75 awards in 47 years). We have however, striven to keep the material and illustrations current, including the first public appearance of the new Outstanding Volunteer Service Medal, albeit in sketch form.

And then there's that ugly word; **MISTEAKS**. Every book in print, probably dating back to the Gutenberg Bible, no matter how high-sounding, brilliantly conceived or well-intentioned, is bound to possess its share of factual errors and mispelled words. Owing to the long interval necessary to produce color illustrations, a few errors did creep in but were not identified in time to meet the publication date. However, the accompanying text portions include the appropriate corrections. If any other errors are detected, please accept our apologies and the assurance that these will be rectified in future editions. In this spirit, we will start the ball rolling by pointing out that the words "MISTEAKS" and "mispelled" in the first sentence of this paragraph are both misspelled.

Col. (Ret.) Frank C. Foster
Fairview House
Fountain Inn, SC
December, 1993

BACKGROUND OF UNITED STATES AWARDS

The Andre Medal awarded to patriots Van Wert, Paulding and Williams by Congress in 1780.

AMERICAN REVOLUTION - The chronicle of military decorations in the United States begins early in the American Revolution when Congress voted to award gold medals to outstanding military leaders. The first such medal was struck to honor George Washington for his service in driving the British from Boston in 1776. Similar medals were bestowed upon General Horatio Gates for his victory at the Battle of Saratoga and Captain John Paul Jones after his famous naval engagement with the Serapis in 1779. Unlike present practice, however, these were large, presentation medals not designed to be worn on the military uniform. Interestingly, once the dies were cut, many copies were manufactured and distributed as commemorative medals to instill patriotic pride in the new country's victories. As a matter of interest, many of these early commemorative medallions are still being struck and offered for sale by the U. S. Mint.

The "Andre" Medal broke the custom of restricting the award of medals to successful senior officers and is doubly unique in that it was designed for wear around the neck. The medal was presented by Congress in 1780 to the three enlisted men who captured Major John Andre with the plans to the West Point fortifications in his boot.

In August, 1782, George Washington established the Badge of Military Merit, the first U.S. decoration which had general application to all enlisted men, and one which he hoped would inaugurate a permanent awards system. At the same time, he expressed his fundamental awards philosophy when he issued an order from his headquarters at Newburgh, New York, which read:

"The General, ever desirous to cherish a virtuous ambition in his soldiers, as well as foster and encourage every species of military merit, directs that whenever any singularly meritorious action is performed, the author of it shall be permitted to wear on his facings, over his left breast, the figure of a heart in purple cloth, or silk, edged with narrow lace or binding. Not only instances of unusual gallantry, but also of extraordinary fidelity and essential service in any way shall meet with a due reward...the road to glory in a patriotic army and a free country is thus opened to all. This order is also to have retrospect to the earliest days of the war, and to be considered a permanent one."

Although special and commemorative medals had been awarded previously, until this point no decoration had been established which honored the private soldier with a reward for special merit. The wording of the order is worth careful study. The object was "to cherish a virtuous ambition" and "to foster and encourage every species of military merit." Note also, that Washington appreciated that every kind of service was important by proposing to reward, "not only instances of unusual gallantry, but also of extraordinary fidelity and essential service in any way." And finally, the wonderfully democratic sentence, "the road to glory in a patriotic army and free country is thus opened to all."

Coming, as it did, however, almost a year after Cornwallis' surrender at Yorktown, the message was never given widespread distribution and, as a result, there were only three known recipients of this badge, Sergeants Elijah Churchill, William Brown and Daniel Bissell. Unfortunately, after the Revolution, the award fell into disuse and disappeared for 150 years.

1782 Badge of Military Merit and 1932 Purple Heart.

However, it did not die, primarily due to the efforts of the Army's then Chief of Staff, General Douglas MacArthur, (and, by no accident, one of its first recipients). On the 200th anniversary of Washington's birth, February 22, 1932, the War Department announced that:

"By order of the President of the United States, the Purple Heart, established by Gen. George Washington at Newburgh, New York.....is hereby revived out of respect to his memory and military achievements."

Washington's "figure of a heart in purple" was retained as the medal's central theme and embellished with Washington's likeness and his coat of arms. The words "For Military Merit" appear on the reverse as a respectful reference to its worthy predecessor.

CIVIL WAR - In the eighty years after the Revolution, the United States engaged in at least two major conflicts with foreign nations (War of 1812, War with Mexico), but no attempt was made to revive or re-establish a comprehensive awards program. The Certificate of Merit was established by the Army in 1847 to reward soldiers who distinguished themselves in battle, but this was not translated into medallic form until 1905. In 1861, the Medal of Honor was established for enlisted personnel of the U.S. Navy, followed the next year by the creation of its Army counterpart for NCO's and private soldiers. Officers were made eligible for the award in later years.

1862 Army MOH

1861 Navy MOH

SPANISH AMERICAN WAR - For nearly twenty years, the Medal of Honor remained the sole American military award of any kind. Although the Navy and Marine Corps had authorized the first Good Conduct Medals in the 1880's, it was not until the eve of the 20th Century that a host of medals were authorized to commemorate the events surrounding the Spanish-American War. This was future President Theodore Roosevelt's "Bully Little War" that produced seven distinct medals for only four months of military action.

The first of these was the medal to commemorate the victory of the naval forces under the command of Commodore Dewey over the Spanish fleet at Manila Bay. This award was notable as it was the first such medal in U.S. history to be awarded to all officers and enlisted personnel present during a specific military expedition.

When Roosevelt, an ardent supporter of the military, ultimately reached the White House, he took it upon himself to legislate for the creation of medals to honor all those who had served in America's previous conflicts. Thus, by 1908, the U.S. had authorized campaign medals, some retroactive, for the Civil War, Indian Wars, War with Spain, Philippine Insurrection and China Relief Expedition of 1900-01. While the Services used the same ribbons, different medals were struck. Also, the custom of wearing service ribbons on the tunic was adopted during this same time frame (using different precedences). Thus, the Services managed to establish the principle of independence in the creation and wearing of awards that is virtually unchanged today.

WORLD WAR I - At the time of the U.S. entry into World War I, the Medal of Honor , Certificate of Merit and Navy/Marine Good Conduct Medal still represented America's entire inventory of personal decorations. This presented the twin dangers that the Medal of Honor might be cheapened by being awarded too often and that other deeds of valor might go unrecognized. By 1918, popular agitation forced the authorization of two new awards, the Army's Distinguished Service Cross and Distinguished Service Medal, created by Executive Order in 1918. In the same year, the traditional U.S. refusal to permit the armed forces to accept foreign decorations was rescinded, allowing military personnel to accept awards from the grateful Allied governments. In 1919, the Navy created the Navy Cross and its own Distinguished Service Medal for Navy and Marine Corps personnel.

Army Distinguished Service Cross

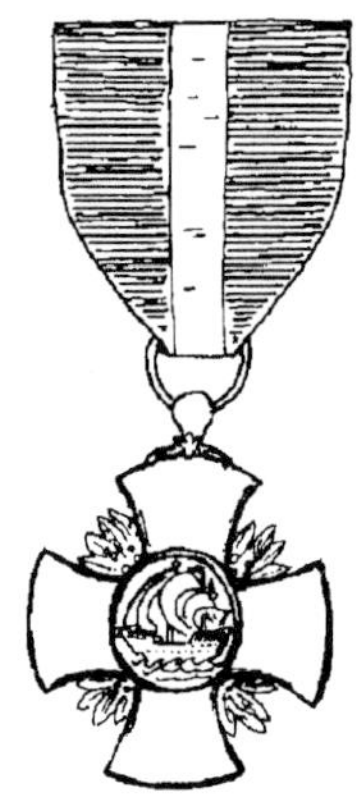

Navy Cross

The issuance of the World War I Victory Medal established another precedent, that of wearing clasps with the names of individual battles on the suspension ribbon of a campaign medal. This was an ongoing practice in many countries, most notably the British and French, since the 19th Century. When the ribbon bar alone was worn, each clasp was represented by a small (3/16" diameter) bronze star. Fourteen such clasps were adopted along with five clasps to denote service in specific countries. However, the latter were issued only if no battle clasp was earned. Only one service clasp could be issued to any individual and they were not represented by a small (3/16") bronze star on the ribbon bar.

It is a final irony that the British, who were the greatest proponents of the practice, never issued a single bar with their own version of the Victory Medal.

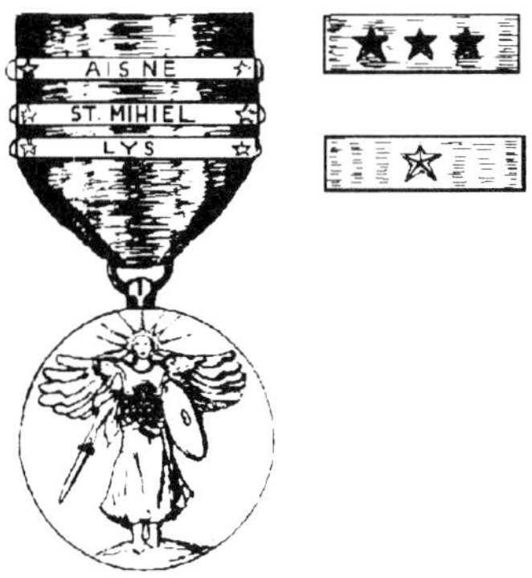

World War I Victory Medal with Ribbon Bars

During this same period, the Army used a 3/16" diameter silver star to indicate a citation for gallantry during any previous campaign, dating back to the Civil War. An officer or enlisted man so cited was also presented with a Silver Star citation, which evolved into the Silver Star Medal in 1932.

Between the two World Wars, American troops were dispatched to such areas as Haiti, Nicaragua and China to quell rebellions and deal with civil unrest and appropriate medals were authorized to commemorate these events.

WORLD WAR II - On September 8, 1939, in response to the growing threat of involvement in World War II, the President proclaimed a National Emergency in order to increase the size of the U.S. military forces. For the first time, a peacetime service award, the American Defense Service Medal, was authorized for wear by those personnel who served in the military, prior to the attack on Pearl Harbor on December 7, 1941.

The onset of America's participation in World War II saw a significant increase in both personal decorations and campaign medals. Since U.S. forces were serving all over the world, a campaign medal was designed for each major (and carefully defined) area. The three medals for the American, Asiatic-Pacific and European-African-Middle Eastern Campaigns encompassed the globe. However, the World War I practice of using campaign bars was discarded in favor of 3/16" bronze stars that could denote any military endeavor, from a major invasion, to a submarine war patrol.

World War II, also introduced the first (and only!) service medal unique to female military personnel. Known as the Women's Army Corps Service Medal, it was authorized for service in both the W.A.C. and its predecessor, the Women's Army Auxiliary Corps. In addition, the war saw the large scale award of foreign medals and decorations to American servicemen. The Philippine Government, for one, authorized awards to commemorate the Defense and Liberation of their island country. The first foreign award designed strictly for units, the Philippine Presidential Unit Citation, patterned after a similar American award, was also approved for wear by American forces at this time. In the European Theater, France and Belgium made many presentations of their War Medals (Croix de Guerre) to U. S. military personnel.

Asiatic-Pacific and European-African- Middle Eastern Campaign Medals.

The next mid-war period, from 1945 to 1950, saw the introduction of two counterparts of previous World War I awards, the Victory and Occupation Medals. This time, no bars or clasps were authorized for the Victory Medal, but bars were issued with the Occupation Medal to denote the recipient's area of service.

KOREA - The Korean conflict, fought under the United Nations banner, added two new medals to the inventory. The first was the Korean Service Medal, which continued the practice of using 3/16" bronze stars on the ribbon to denote major engagements. The second, the National Defense Service Medal, set another record when it was later reinstated for the Vietnam and Gulf Wars to become the most awarded medal in U.S. history. Some units received the Korean Presidential Unit Citation and all participants were awarded the United Nations Service Medal, but no medal was ever issued by the South Korean Government to U.S. and other foreign troops.

U.S. Korean Service Medal

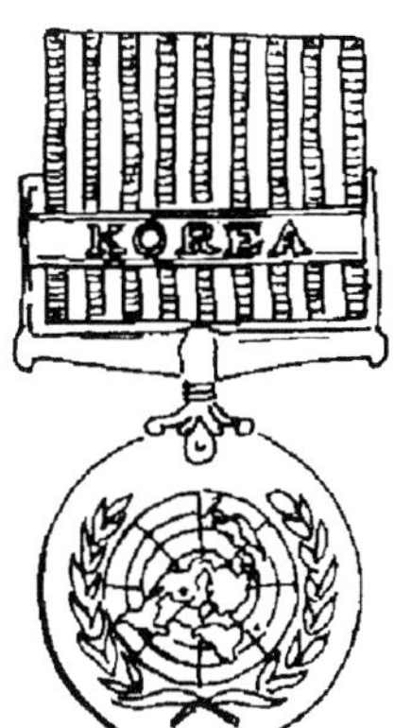

UN Korean Service Medal

In the late 1950's and early 1960's, another substantial increase in awards took place as the Air Force, a separate Service since 1947, created a flood of unique honors to replace their Army counterparts.

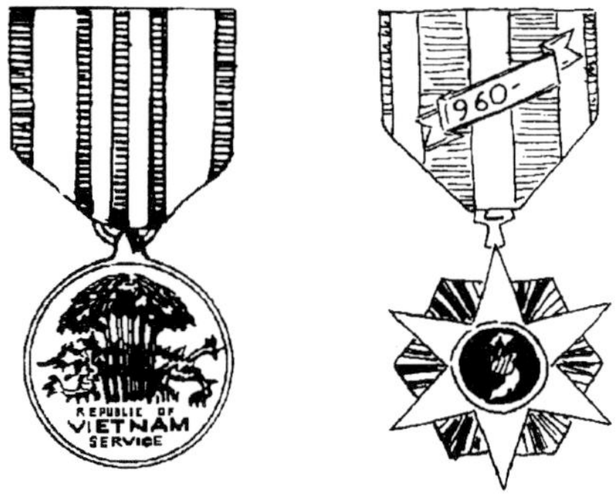

U.S. Vietnam and RVN Campaign Medals.

VIETNAM - The first American advisors in the Republic of South Vietnam, were awarded the new Armed Forces Expeditionary Medal which was created in 1961 to cover campaigns for which no specific medal was instituted. However, as the U.S. involvement in the Vietnamese conflict grew, a unique award, the Vietnam Service Medal was authorized, thus giving previous recipients of the Expeditionary Medal the option of which medal to accept. The Government also authorized the acceptance of the Republic of Vietnam Campaign Medal by all who served for six months in-country, the surrounding waters or the air after 1960.

After Vietnam, many new decorations, medals and ribbons came into being as the Department of Defense and the individual Services developed a complete structure to reward performance from the newest enlistee to the most senior Pentagon Staffer. Some of the awards, such as the Army Service Ribbon and the Air Force Training Ribbon have little meaning, except to give the recruit something to wear on his chest. Conversely, the Achievement and Commendation Medals provide a useful means for a field commander to recognize younger individuals for outstanding performance.

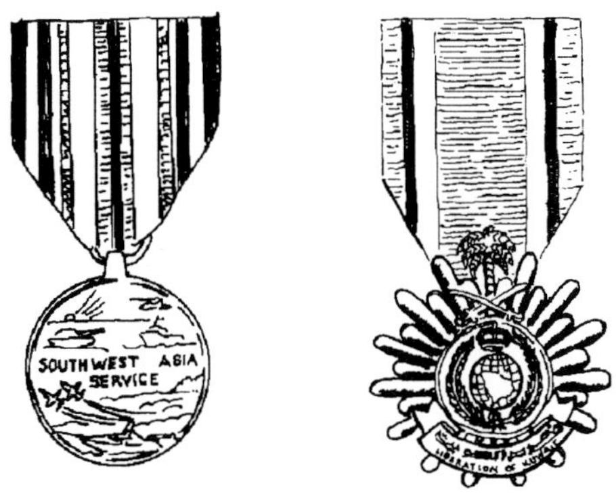

U.S. Southwest Service Medal and Saudi Arabian Medal for Liberation of Kuwait

GULF WAR - The conflict in the Gulf, as previously noted, saw the reinstitution of the National Defense Service Medal (this time it also covered the Reserves) and the creation of the Southwest Asia Service Medal for the personnel in theater. The Department of Defense also approved the wear of the Saudi Arabian Medal for the Liberation of Kuwait, which probably wins the award as the "Most Colorful Medal" hanging on any military chest.

TYPE OF AWARDS - The terms, "Decoration" and "Medal" are used almost interchangeably today, but there was once a recognizable distinction between them. Decorations, awarded for acts of valor and meritorious service, usually had distinctive (and often unique) outlines. Medals, which were awarded for participation in specific battles or campaigns, normally came in basic round. The fact that some very prestigious awards have the word "medal" in their titles (e.g.: Medal of Honor, Marine Corps Brevet Medal, Distinguished Service Medal, etc.) can cause some confusion to the novice.

Another type of award is a badge, indicating special proficiency in specific areas, such as marksmanship. The Services have also developed a system by which entire units, such as an Army Battalion or a Navy ship can be recognized for outstanding performance in the field. Members of the cited unit are entitled to wear an appropriate insignia representing the award (e.g.: Presidential Unit Citation, Navy Unit Commendation) or the French Fourragere, worn in perpetuity by members of many Army and Marine units to honor it's award during one of the World Wars. .

PURPOSE - It is the purpose of this book to provide the reader with a clear road map of U.S. military awards and decorations. Starting on Page 9, details involved in claiming, wearing and displaying military awards are presented. The narrative continues on Page 17, with the personal decorations starting with the Medal of Honor and proceeding through the various levels of the "Pyramid of Honor". Next in order, are the Good Conduct, Special Service and Reserve Meritorious Awards, followed by the service medals in chronological order from 1939 to the present.

The Marksmanship medals and ribbons of the Navy, Coast Guard and Air Force are presented next (note that both the Army and Marine Corps award metal badges for shooting excellence, but these are beyond the scope of this book). This is followed by sections on the awards of various Foreign governments to U.S. personnel, ribbons which have no associated medals ("ribbon-only" awards) and, finally, U.S. and foreign unit awards.

Finally, to complete the awards picture, sections depicting the proper wear of ribbons, describing devices and attachments, and attempting to explain the details of the U. S. awards system are included.

From the earliest orders of knighthood to the present day commendations, the purpose of awards has always been two-fold; the first is to promote good service, pride and courageous conduct among military personnel. The second is to create a mystique that will surround these symbols of a nation's appreciation, and thus provides recognition for the recipients, their comrades, and their families.

Even the service medals and ribbons, the so-called, "I Was There and Survived" awards have an important purpose. The display on a serviceman's chest can tell a commander at a glance the level of experience possessed by his subordinates. When a commander reviews his officers and NCO's, it only takes a minute or so to evaluate their backgrounds and predict performance from their ribbons.

It is, therefore, the authors' hope that this book will allow the reader, whether novice or veteran, to gain a new understanding of American awards, their evolution and history up to the present time.

3. CLAIMING U. S. MILITARY MEDALS FROM THE U. S. GOVERNMENT

Veterans of any U. S. military service may request replacement of medals which have been lost, stolen, destroyed or rendered unfit through no fault of the recipient. Requests may also be filed for awards that were earned but, for any reason, were never issued to the service member. The next-of-kin of deceased veterans may also make the same request.

AIR FORCE - The Air Force processes requests for medals through the National Personnel Records Center, which determines eligibility through the information in the veteran's records. Once verified, a notification of entitlement is forwarded to Randolph Air Force Base, Texas, from which the medals are mailed to the requestor. To request medals earned while in the Air Force or its predecessor, the Army Air Corps, veterans or their next-of-kin should write to:

National Personnel Records Center
(Military Personnel Records)
9700 Page Boulevard
St. Louis, MO 63132-5100

ARMY - The National Personnel Records Center does not determine eligibility for awards issued by the other services. If the person served in the Army, the request should be sent to:

U. S. Army Reserve Personnel Center
Attn. DARP-VSE-A
9700 Page Boulevard
St. Louis, MO 63132-5100

ALL NAVAL SERVICES - Requests pertaining to persons who served in the Navy, Marine Corps or Coast Guard should be sent to:

Navy Liaison Office (Navy Medals)
Room 3475
9700 Page Avenue
St. Louis, MO 63132-5100

It is recommended that requestors use Standard Form 180, *Request Pertaining to Military Records* when applying. Forms are available from offices of the Department of Veterans Affairs (VA) or photocopy the example on page 75. If the Standard Form 180 is not used, a letter may be sent, but it must include: the veteran's full name used while in service, the branch of service, approximate dates of service and service number. The letter should indicate if the request is for a specific medal(s) or for all medals earned. The letter must be signed by the veteran or his next-of-kin, indicating the relationship to the deceased.

It is also helpful to include copies of any military service documents that indicate eligibility for medals, such as military orders or the report of separation (DD Form 214 or its earlier equivalent). This is especially important if the request pertains to one of the millions of veteran's whose original records were lost in a fire at the National Personnel Records Center in 1973. The destroyed records involved all veterans who were discharged from the Army or Army Air Corps before 1960, or from the Air Force before 1964 and whose last names fall alphabetically between Hubbard (James E.) and Z. Although the requested medals can often be issued on the basis of alternate records, the documents sent in with the request are sometimes the only means of determining proper eligibility.

Finally, requestors should exercise extreme patience. It may take several months or, in some cases, a year to determine eligibility and dispatch the appropriate medals.

The Bronze Star (Decoration) , and The National Defense Service Medal (Medal)

4. PROPER WEAR OF U. S. AWARDS

GENERAL CONSIDERATIONS

One of the earliest principles taught to the new recruit is that the uniform must always be worn properly. This applies to every item placed on that uniform, most especially to ribbons and medals. Decorations and awards must always be worn on the proper occasions, on the right uniform and in the correct order of precedence. The following pages outline the general rules for wear as prescribed by each Service. Regardless of branch, medals should always be clean and ribbons unsoiled. Items that are not absolutely spotless should <u>not</u> be worn, but should be redraped or reribboned immediately.

For active duty personnel, awards are worn per the applicable regulations on dress and service uniforms during normal working hours and while off-duty. Military personnel may also wear miniature medals on cilivian evening attire at formal social functions.

National Guard and Reserve personnel follow the same general rules when in uniform. Those on the retired lists are also authorized to wear their uniforms and decorations on ceremonial occasions. This means a special event essentially military in nature at which the uniform is more appropriate than civilian dress. Examples of these are military balls, parades, weddings, funerals, memorial services, military association meetings and specific patriotic events. Military retirees may wear the uniform of their grade and branch at the time of retirement. However, military and civilian dress may not be mixed.

Retired personnel and former soldiers may wear either full size or miniature medals, on appropriate civilian clothing including clothes designed for veteran's and patriotic organizations on Veteran's Day, Memorial Day, and Armed Forces Day as well as at formal occasions of ceremony and social functions of a military nature.

WEAR ON CIVILIAN CLOTHES

There are two styles of awards that may be displayed on civilian clothes. The first is the small enameled lapel pin that represents the ribbon bar of a single decoration (usually the highest award or one having special meaning to the wearer). This is worn in the left lapel buttonhole of the civilian suit jacket. Many well-known veterans now in positions of leadership like Senator Bob Dole, a World War II Purple Heart recipient, wear such a lapel pin.

The other award style is the miniature medal, worn on the black or white dinner jacket at social functions. The rule of wear for these items is quite simple; if the lapel is wide enough, then they are worn on the lapel**. If the lapel is too narrow (e.g.: the shawl lapel on a tuxedo), the mini-medals are worn so that the bottom row of pendants just covers the top of the left breast pocket. No badges are ever worn on civilian dress.

** These are centered on the left lapel, 1/2 inch below the notch or 1 inch below the end of the collar gorge.

4. WEARING RIBBONS & MEDALS

UNITED STATES ARMY

Wear Of Service Ribbons - Ribbons may be worn on the Army green, blue and white uniform coats. The ribbons are worn in one or more rows in order of precedence with either no space or 1/8 inch between rows. No more than four ribbons to a row. The top row is centered or aligned to left edge of the row underneath, whichever looks the best. Unit awards are centered above the right breast pocket.

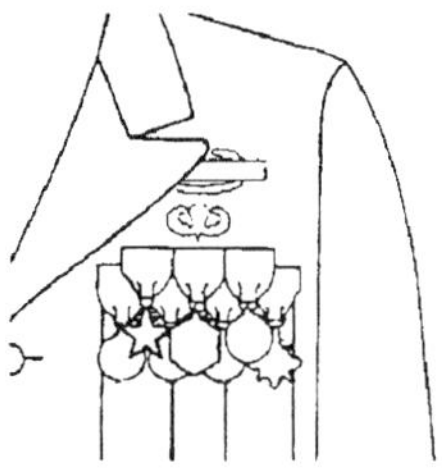

Wear Of Full Size Decorations & Service Medals - Decorations and service medals may be worn on the Army blue or white uniform after retreat and by enlisted personnel on the dress green uniform for social functions. The medals are mounted in order of precedence, in rows with not more than four medals in a row. The top row cannot have more medals than the one below. Rows are separated by 1/8 inch. Medals may not overlap (as Navy and Marines do), so normally there are only three to a row due to the size of the coat. Service and training ribbons are not worn with full size medals.

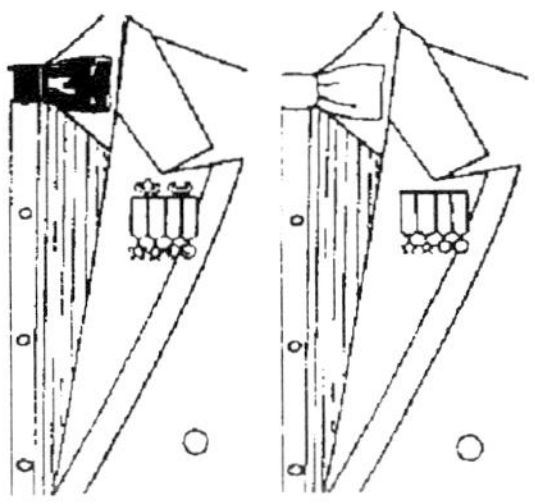

Wear Of Miniature Decorations & Service Medals - Miniature medals are scaled down replicas of full size medals. Only miniature medals are authorized for wear on the mess and evening uniform jackets (and with the blue and white uniform after retreat on formal occasions.)

Miniature medals are mounted on bars with the order of precedence from the wearer's right to left. The medals are mounted side by side if there are four or less. They may be overlapped up to 50% when five, six or seven are in a row. Overlapping is equal for all medals with the right one fully displayed. When two or more rows are worn, the bottom pendants must be fully visible.

UNITED STATES NAVY

(The USCG Generally Follows USN Guidelines)

Wear Of Service Ribbons - Wear up to 3 in a row, if more than three ribbons wear in horizontal rows of three each. The top row contains the lessor number, centered above the row below. No spaces between ribbon rows. Rows of ribbons covered by coat lapel may contain two ribbons each and be aligned. Wear ribbons with lower edge of bottom row centered 1/4 inch above left breast and parallel to the deck.

USCG member option is to either wear senior three ribbons or all ribbons when they are covered by lapel by 1/3 or more. Rows can be decreased to 2 or 1 if all ribbons are worn in this situation.

Wear Of Full Size Decorations And Service Medals - Wear large medals on full dress uniforms. Align bottom row same as ribbon bars. All rows may contain maximum of 3 medals side by side or up to 5 overlapping. Overlapping is proportional with inboard medal showing in full. Mount medals so they cover suspension ribbon of the medal below.

Wear Of Miniature Medals - Wear miniature medals with all formal and dinner dress uniforms. Place holding bar of lowest row of miniatures 3 inches below the notch, centered on the lapel. Center the holding bar immediately above the left breast pocket on the blue and white service coat. You may wear up to five miniature medals in a row with no overlap on the dinner jacket, center up to 3 miniature medals on the lapel. Position 4 or more miniatures at the inner edge of the lapel extending beyond the lapel to the body of the jacket.

UNITED STATES MARINE CORPS

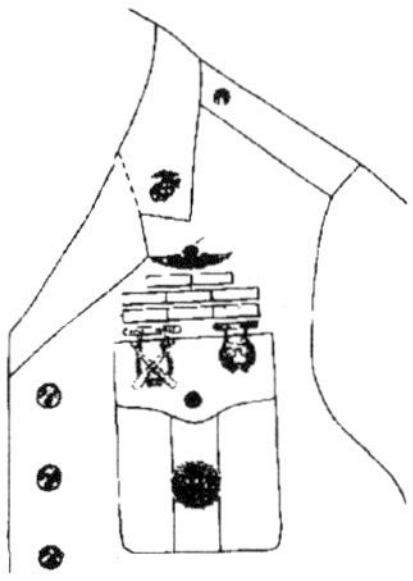

Wear Of Service Ribbons - Ribbons are authorized on Marine dress "B", dress "A" or shirts when prescribed as an outer garment. They are normally worn in rows of 3 or rows of 4 when displaying a large number of awards. If the lapel conceals any ribbons, they may be placed in successively decreasing rows (ie: 4, 3, 2, 1). All aligned vertically on center, except if the top row can be altered to present the neatest appearance. Ribbon rows may be spaced 1/8 inch apart or together. Ribbon bars are centered 1/8 inch above the upper left pocket. When marksmanship badges are worn, the ribbon bars are 1/8 inch above them.

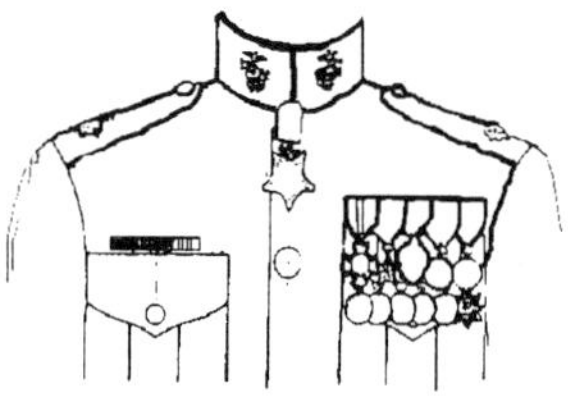

Full Size Medals - Marines wear up to 4 medals side by side on a 3 1/4 inch bar. A maximum of 7 medals may be overlapped (not to exceed 50% with the right or inboard medal shown in full). Full size medals are worn on blue or white dress coat centered on the left breast pocket with the upper edge of the holding bar on line midway between the 1st and 2nd button of the coat. When large medals are worn, all unit citations and ribbons with no medal authorized are centered over the right breast pocket the bottom edge 1/8 inch above the top of the pocket.

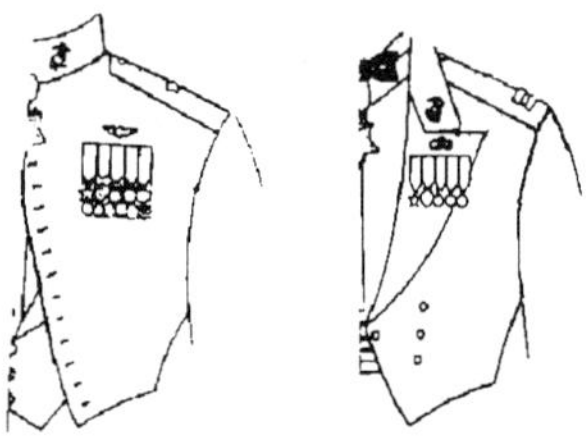

Wear Of Miniature Medals - When miniature medals are worn, no ribbons will be worn. On evening dress jackets miniature medals will be centered on the left front jacket panel midway between the inner edge and the left armhole seam, with the top of the bar on line with the 2nd blind button hole. On mess dress and SNCO's evening and mess dress the miniature medals are centered on the left lapel with the top of the holding bar 1 inch below the lapel notch.

UNITED STATES AIR FORCE

Wear Of Service Ribbons - Ribbons are worn on service dress and blue shirt. Ribbons are normally worn in rows of three with the bottom bar centered and resting on the top edge of the pocket. Ribbons may be worn four-in-a-row with the left edge of the ribbons aligned with the left edge of pocket to keep lapel from covering ribbons. There is no space between rows of ribbons.

Full Size Medals - Normally worn three to a row, but may be overlapped up to five medals on a 2 3/4 inch holding bar. No medal should be overlapped more than 50% and the medal nearest the lapel should be fully exposed. Six medals should be displayed in two rows, three over three. Regular size medals are worn on the service dress and ceremonial dress uniforms with the medal portion of the bottom row immediately above the top of the pocket button.

Miniature Medals - Miniature Medals are worn on the blue mess dress or on formal dress. The miniatures are centered between lapel and arm seam and midway between top shoulder seam and top button of jacket. If more than four miniatures, the wearer has the option of mounting up to seven by overlapping or going to a 2nd bar. Seven is the maximum on one bar, however, many in the Air Force prefer only a maximum of four to a bar.

5. HOW TO DISPLAY YOUR MEDALS

DISPLAYING MILITARY AWARDS

In the United States, it is quite rare for an individual to wear full-size medals once no longer on active duty. Unfortunately, many veterans who leave the service, return to civilian life with little concern for the state of their awards. In the euphoria of the moment, medals are tucked away in corners or children play with them, causing irreparable damge to these noble mementos of a man's or woman's patroitic deeds. This is a highly regrettable practice, since awards reflect the veteran's part in American History and are totally unique and personal to each family.

The most appropriate step is to mount the medals for permanent display in home or office, reflecting the individual's patroitism and the service rendered the United States. However, there are very few first class companies in the United States, like Spink's of London, who possess the expertise to properly prepare and mount awards and other personal militaria. The following pages provide examples of the formats, mounting methods and configurations employed by Medals of America in Fountain Inn, South Carolina to display military decorations. The examples range from a single medal to a dozen.

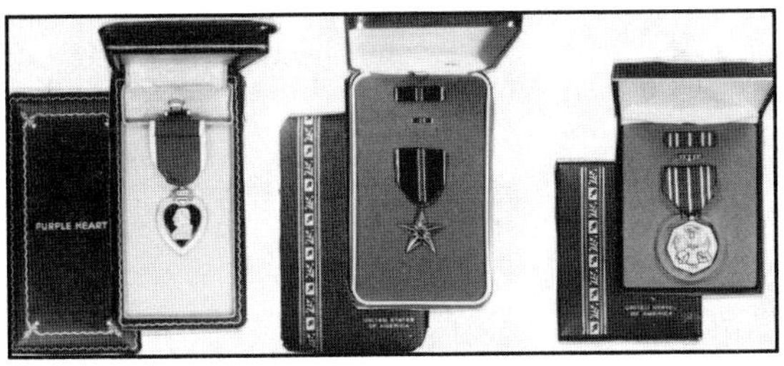

Decorations are usually awarded in a presentation set which normally consists of a medal, ribbon bar and lapel pin, all contained in a special case. During World War II, the name of the decoration was stamped in gold on the front of the case. However, as budget considerations assumed greater importance, this practice was gradually phased out and replaced by a standard case with "United States of America" emblazoned on the front.

At the present time, the more common decorations, (e.g., Achievement and Commendation Medals), come in small plastic cases, suitable only for initial presentation and storage of the medal. Using this case in its open position for prolonged display exposes the entire presentation set to dust, acids and other atmospheric contaminants which can cause tarnish and/or serious discoloration.

Outside the case, medals and ribbons should be handled as little as possible, since oils and dirt on the hands can cause oxidation on the pendant and staining of the ribbon.

The most effective method of protecting awards involves the use of a shadow box or glass display case with at least 1/2 inch between the medals and the glass. This provides a three dimensional view and protects the medal display in a dust-free environment. Cases which press the medals and ribbons against the glass can disfigure the ribbon, cause discoloration and, in some extreme cases, damage the medal.

The greatest mistake an ordinary frame shop can make is in the actual process of mounting the medals. They often clip off prongs or pins on the back of a medal to ease the task of gluing the medal to a flat surface. The physical alteration destroys the integrity of the medal and the use of glues ruins the back of the ribbon and medal. The net result, ignoring the intrinsic value of the piece, is serious damage to a valued heirloom and keepsake.

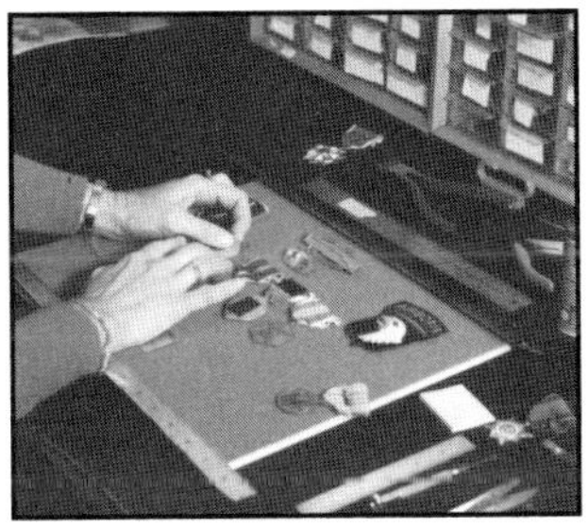

The best way to mount medals is in a wooden case especially designed for that purpose. They can be obtained either with a fold-out easel back for placement on a table, desk or mantle, or with a notched hook on the rear of the wooden frame for hanging on a wall. The case should also have brass turnbuckles on the back to facilitate removal of the mounting board for close examination of the medals or rearrangement of the displayed items.

The mounting board is absolutely critical. Velvet, flannel and old uniforms, just don't do the job. A first class mounting system starts with acid-free Befang or Gator board at least 1/4 inch thick. This board is very sturdy, being composed of two layers of hard, white paper board sandwiched around a foam core. Over this, a high quality velour-type material to which velcro will adhere is glued and pressed down evenly. The medals are mounted using velcro tape; one piece over the ribbon mounting pin and one, about the size of a nickel, on the medal back. The velcro locks the medal very firmly into place without causing any damage and alleviates the need to cut off the pin backs. Badges or ribbon bars with pin backs can be mounted by pressing the prongs through the fabric into the gator board, which moulds around the prongs. A little velcro tape on the back of the pronged device adds extra holding power.

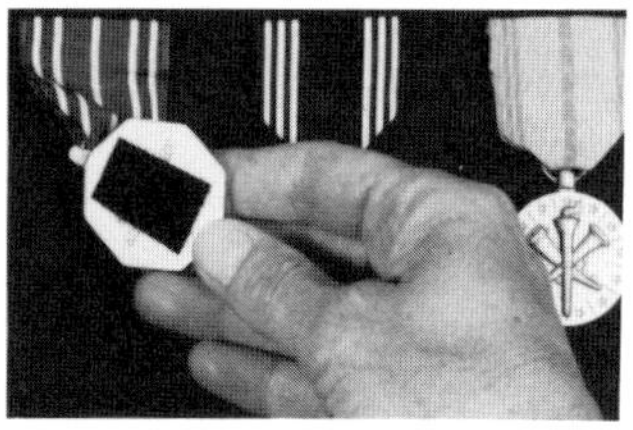

Patches, brass plates, dog tags and other mementos can easily be added this way. The great beauty of this method is found not only in its eye appeal, but also that one can add to the display or rearrange the existing contents by gently peeling the medal off as simply as opening a velcro zipper. Prong devices can also be moved easily, since the foam core closes in behind the prong as it is removed, thus effectively sealing the hole once more.

The final element in the process is the frame itself. While oak and other heavy woods make very handsome pieces of furniture, they are not a good choice for a frame. The frame's weight puts a great strain on modern plasterboard walls when an extensive medal display is attached via standard hooks and nails. In addition, handling a heavy frame by very young or very old hands increases the chance it could be accidentally dropped. For these reasons, frames should be milled from a lightweight wood with good staining characteristics. Bass wood is considered the best for the purpose and some poplar is acceptable. Metal frames, on the other hand, should be avoided, owing to their heavy weight and to the bright coloring which can conflict with the patina of the medals. Finally, the wood stain, (e.g., walnut stain), should reflect a rich, warm glow to properly envelop and enhance the medal display.

A unique example of using ribbons, miniatures, medals and special badges.

An essential part of the display case is the brass plate which provides the key information pertaining to the recipient of the displayed awards. This is definitely a place where one should <u>not</u> cut corners. A bargain basement brass or gold colored plastic nameplate will cheapen and distract from an otherwise elegant display case. Conversely, a high quality brass plate with good quality engraving will forever enhance the dignity of the medal display.

Whenever possible, the engraved letters should be blackened to provide enhanced contrast and visibility. The plate should, as a minimum, contain the full name, assigned unit and time frame. Other useful items are rank, service number and branch of the service if space permits. The contents of a nameplate are obviously a personal preference, but experience has shown that a limit of four or five lines can enhance and compliment the display, while greater numbers are a distraction.

Below and on the next page, are some examples of different display cases. The display of mounted miniature medals shown at right, is called a "convertible mount", since the entire group can be removed for wear. The flag case display below, allows a deceased veteran's flag, medals and photograph to be displayed as a lasting memorial.

This Air Force pilot's awards from Southwest Asia are mounted in a classic group of five. One more medal or badge requires a larger frame to prevent crowding.

These two cases show how a single or a few medals can be mounted in a handsome display.

A classic display of a WW II veteran's awards using his division patch as a focal point.

This Vietnam veteran used both of his combat patches so the overall composition is a nicely balanced inverted "V".

This WW II Navy veteran uses his rating badge as a very effective focal point.

This Korean War Marine uses his combat patch, and dress collar insigina over the medals . The small rank badge and shooting badges flanking the name plate present a wonderful picture of his military service.

World War II Army Air Corps Display

6. U. S. Military Awards

THE PYRAMID OF HONOR

The military awards system of the United States, described in the introduction, has evolved into a structured program often called the "Pyramid of Honor".The design of which is to reward services ranging from heroism on the battlefield to superior performance of non-combat duties and even includes the completion of entry level training.

Far from being disturbed by the award proliferation, the Armed Services have embraced Napoleon's concept of liberally awarding medals to enhance morale and esprit de corps. This expanded and specifically-tailored awards program is generally very popular in the all-volunteer armed forces. The program has played a significant part in junior officers and enlisted personnel morale, job performance, recruitment and re-enlistments.

The decorations and awards which represent the rich United States military heritage from 1939 onward are presented on the following pages in an overall order of precedence (individual service orders of precedence start on Page 38.). These awards paint a wonderful portrait of this country's dedication to the ideals of freedom and the honors and sacrifices required of the military to support those ideals.

THE MEDAL OF HONOR

In a country whose Government is based on a totally democratic society, it is fitting that the first medal to reward meritorious acts on the field of battle should be for private soldiers and seamen (although extended in later years to officers).

The Congressional Medal of Honor (referred to universally as the "Medal of Honor" in all statutes, awards manuals and uniform regulations) was born in conflict, steeped in controversy during its early years and finally emerged, along with Britain's Victoria Cross and France's Legion of Honor, as one of the premier awards for bravery in the world.

The medal is actually a statistical anomaly proving the unlikely equation that "Three equals One". Although there are three separate medals representing America's highest reward for bravery (illustrated as items 1, 2 and 3 on the next page), there is now only a single set of directives governing the award of this, the most coveted of all U.S. decorations.

The medal was created during the Civil War as a reward for "gallantry in action and other soldierlike qualities" ("...seamanlike qualities..." in the case of the Navy). However, the reference to "other qualities" led to many awards for actions which would seem less than heroic, including the bestowal of 864 awards upon the entire membership of the 27th Maine Volunteer Infantry for merely reenlisting.

The inconsistencies in those and other dubious cases, were apparently resolved in the early 20th Century when 910 names were removed from the lists (including the 864 to the 27th Maine). At the same time, the statutes which govern the award of the medal were revised to reflect the present-day criteria of "Gallantry and intrepidity at the risk of his/her life above and beyond the call of duty".

ARMY MEDAL OF HONOR

The 1862 Army Medal of Honor was redesigned in 1904 and patented by the War Department. Since the original medal was copied by veterans groups, the patent insures the exclusivity of the design.

The medal, a five pointed golden star lays over a green enamel laurel wreath. The center of the star depicts Minerva, goddess of righteous war and wisdom. Her portrait is encircled by the words, "United States of America". The back of the medal is inscribed, "The Congress to" , with a place for the recipient's name. The medal hangs from a bar enscribed "Valor", which is held by an American Eagle with laurel leaves (peace) in its right claw and arrows (war) in its left. The eagle is fastened by a hook to a light blue silk pad embroidered with 13 stars.

NAVY MEDAL OF HONOR

The 1861 Navy Medal of Honor, was redesigned by Tiffany in 1917, but reverted to the basic 1861 design in 1942, with the addition of a neck ribbon. The original design is a five point bronze star, with Minerva repulsing discord. The back of the medal is engraved, "Personal Valor", with room for the recipient's name, rank, ship or unit and date. The medal hangs from the flukes of an anchor, which is attached to the neck ribbon.

AIR FORCE MEDAL OF HONOR

Congress established the Air Force Medal of Honor on July 6, 1960. Before this, airmen received the Army Medal of Honor. The medal design is developed from the Army's and is a five pointed star, with a green enamel laurel wreath. The center shows the Statue of Liberty's head surrounded by 34 stars. The star hangs from a trophy of the Air Force Coat of Arms and is suspended from a bar enscribed, "Valor".

Plate 1. MEDALS OF HONOR

1. MEDAL OF HONOR (ARMY)

For conspicuous gallantry and intrepidity at the risk of life, above and beyond the call of duty, in action involving actual conflict with an opposing armed force.

2. MEDAL OF HONOR (NAVY-MARINE CORPS-COAST GUARD)

For conspicuous gallantry and intrepidity at the risk of life, above and beyond the call of duty, in action involving actual conflict with an opposing armed force.

3. MEDAL OF HONOR (AIR FORCE)

For conspicuous gallantry and intrepidity at the risk of life, above and beyond the call of duty, in action involving actual conflict with an opposing armed force.

Plate 2. U.S. Personal Decorations - Sheet 1

4. Distinguished Service Cross

5. Navy Cross

6. Air Force Cross

7. Defense Distinguished Service Medal

8. Army Distinguished Service Medal

9. Navy Distinguished Service Medal

10. Air Force Distinguished Service Medal

11. Coast Guard Distinguished Service Medal

12. Silver Star

13. Defense Superior Service Medal

14. Legion Of Merit

15. Dist. Flying Cross

United States Personal Decorations

4. Distinguished Service Cross

Service: Army

Instituted: 1918

Criteria: Extraordinary heroism in action against an enemy of the U.S. or while serving with friendly foreign forces

Devices: Bronze, silver oak leaf cluster (28, 32)

Notes: 100 copies of earlier design cross issued with a European-style (unedged) ribbon ("French Cut")

5. Navy Cross

Service: Navy/Marine Corps/Coast Guard

Instituted: 1919

Criteria: Extraordinary heroism in action against an enemy of the U.S. or while serving with friendly foreign forces

Devices: Gold, silver star (66, 70)

Notes: Originally issued with a 1 1/2" wide ribbon

6. Air Force Cross

Service: Air Force

Instituted: 1960

Criteria: Extraordinary heroism in action against an enemy of the U.S. or while serving with friendly foreign forces

Devices: Bronze, silver oak leaf cluster (28, 32)

7. Defense Distinguished Service Medal

Service: All Services (by Secretary of Defense)

Instituted: 1970

Criteria: Exceptionally meritorious service to the United States while assigned to a Joint Activity in a position of unique and great responsibility

Devices: Army/Air Force/ Navy/Marine Corps: bronze & silver oak leaf cluster (29, 33); Coast Guard: gold, silver star (65, 69)
Notes: Coast Guard uses gold star device since the oak leaf cluster may not be worn on its uniform

8. Army Distinguished Service Medal

Service: Army

Instituted: 1918

Criteria: Exceptionally meritorious service to the United States Government in a duty of great responsibility

Devices: Bronze, silver oak leaf cluster (28, 32)

Notes: Originally issued with European (unedged) ribbon ("French Cut")

9. Navy Distinguished Service Medal

Service: Navy/Marine Corps

Instituted: 1919

Criteria: Exceptionally meritorious service to the United States Government in a duty of great responsibility

Devices: Gold, silver star (66, 70)
Notes: 107 copies of earlier medal design issued but later withdrawn. First ribbon design was 1 1/2" wide

10. Air Force Distinguished Service Medal

Service: Air Force

Instituted: 1960

Criteria: Exceptionally meritorious service to the United States Government in a duty of great responsibility

Devices: Bronze, silver oak leaf cluster (28, 32)

Notes: Original design was modified and used as the Airman's Medal

11. Coast Guard Distinguished Service Medal

Service: Coast Guard

Instituted: 1961

Criteria: Exceptionally meritorious service to the United States Government in a duty of great responsibility

Devices: Gold, silver star (66, 70)

Notes: Originally authorized in 1949 but the design was not approved until 1961

12. Silver Star

Service: All Services (originally Army only)

Instituted: 1932

Criteria: Gallantry in action against an armed enemy of the United States or while serving with friendly foreign forces
Devices: Army/Air Force: bronze, silver oak leaf cluster (28, 32); Navy/Marine Corps/Coast Guard: gold, silver star (66, 70)

Notes: Derived from the 3/16" silver "Citation Star" previously worn on Army campaign medals

13. Defense Superior Service Medal

Service: All Services (by Secretary of Defense)

Instituted: 1970

Criteria: Superior meritorious service to the United States while assigned to a Joint Activity in a position of significant responsibility

Devices: Army/Air Force/ Navy/Marine Corps: bronze, silver oak leaf cluster (29, 33); Coast Guard: gold, silver star (65, 69)
Notes: Coast Guard uses gold star device since the oak leaf cluster may not be worn on its uniform

14. Legion of Merit

Service: All Services

Instituted: 1942

Criteria: Exceptionally meritorious conduct in the performance of outstanding services to the United States

Devices: Army/Air Force: bronze, silver oak leaf cluster (28, 32); Navy/Marine Corps/Coast Guard: bronze letter "V" (for valor) (17), gold, silver star (66, 70)
Notes: Issued in four degrees (Legionnaire, Officer, Commander & Chief Commander) to foreign nationals

15. Distinguished Flying Cross

Service: All Services

Instituted: 1926

Criteria: Heroism or extraordinary achievement while participating in aerial flight

Devices: Army/Air Force: bronze, silver oak leaf cluster (28, 32); Navy/Marine Corps: bronze letter "V" (for valor) (17), gold, silver star (66, 70); Coast Guard: gold, silver star (66, 70)

Plate 2. U.S. Personal Decorations - Sheet 2

16. Soldier's Medal

17. Navy and Marine Corps Medal

18. Airman's Medal

19. Coast Guard Medal

20. Gold Lifesaving Medal

21. Bronze Star Medal

22. Purple Heart

23. Defense Meritorious Service Medal

24. Meritorious Service Medal

25. Air Medal

26. Silver Lifesaving Medal

27. Aerial Achievement Medal

United States Personal Decorations (cont'd)

16. Soldier's Medal

Service: Army

Instituted: 1926

Criteria: Heroism not involving actual conflict with an armed enemy of the United States

Devices: Bronze, silver oak leaf cluster (28, 32)

17. Navy and Marine Corps Medal

Service: Navy/Marine Corps

Instituted: 1942

Criteria: Heroism not involving actual conflict with an armed enemy of the United States

Devices: Gold, silver star (66, 70)

18. Airman's Medal

Service: Air Force

Instituted: 1960

Criteria: Heroism involving voluntary risk of life under conditions other than those of actual conflict with an armed enemy

Devices: Bronze, silver oak leaf cluster (28, 32)

Notes: Derived from original design of Air Force Distinguished Service Medal

19. Coast Guard Medal

Service: Coast Guard

Instituted: 1958

Criteria: Heroism not involving actual conflict with an armed enemy of the United States

Devices: Gold, silver star (66, 70)

Notes: Authorized in 1949 but not designed and issued until 1958

20. Gold Life Saving Medal

Service: All Services and Civilians

Instituted: 1874 (modified 1882 and 1946)

Criteria: Heroic conduct at the risk of life during the rescue or attempted rescue of a victim of drowning or shipwreck

Devices: Coast Guard: gold star (66)

Notes: Normally a "Non-Military Decoration" but considered a personal decoration by the Coast Guard. Originally a "table" (non-wearable) medal then worn with a 2" wide ribbon

21. Bronze Star Medal

Service: All Services

Instituted: 1944

Criteria: Heroic or meritorious achievement or service not involving participation in aerial flight

Devices: Army/Air Force: bronze letter "V" (for valor) (17), bronze, silver oak leaf cluster (28, 32); Navy/Marine Corps/Coast Guard: bronze letter "V" (for valor) (17), gold, silver star (66, 70)

Notes: Awarded to World War II holders of Army Combat Infantryman Badge or Combat Medical Badge

22. Purple Heart

Service: All Services (originally Army only)

Instituted: 1932

Criteria: Awarded to any member of the U.S. Armed Forces killed or wounded in an armed conflict

Devices: Army/Air Force: bronze, silver oak leaf cluster (28, 32); Navy/Marine Corps/Coast Guard: gold, silver star (66, 70)

Notes: Wound Ribbon appeared circa 1917-18 but was never officially authorized. (Army used wound chevrons during World War I)

23. Defense Meritorious Service Medal

Service: All Services (by Secretary of Defense)

Instituted: 1977

Criteria: Noncombat meritorious achievement or service while assigned to the Joint Activity

Devices: Army/Air Force/Navy/Marine Corps: bronze, silver oak leaf cluster (29, 33); Coast Guard: gold, silver star (65, 69)

Notes: Coast Guard uses gold star device since the oak leaf cluster may not be worn on its uniform

24. Meritorious Service Medal

Service: All Services

Instituted: 1969

Criteria: Outstanding noncombat meritorious achievement or service to the United States

Devices: Army/Air Force: bronze, silver oak leaf cluster (28, 32); Navy/Marine Corps: gold, silver star (66, 70); Coast Guard: silver letter "O" (14), gold, silver star (66, 70)

25. Air Medal

Service: All Services

Instituted: 1942

Criteria: Heroic actions or meritorious service while participating in aerial flight

Devices: Army: bronze letter "V" (for valor) (17), bronze numeral (25); Air Force: bronze, silver oak leaf cluster (28, 32); Navy/Marine Corps: bronze letter "V" (for valor) (17), bronze numeral (21), gold numeral (26), bronze star (53), gold, silver star (66, 70); Coast Guard: gold, silver star (66, 70)

26. Silver Life Saving Medal

Service: All Services and Civilians

Instituted: 1874 (modified 1882 and 1946)

Criteria: Heroic conduct during rescue or attempted rescue of a victim of drowning or shipwreck

Devices: Coast Guard: gold star (66)

Notes: Normally a "Non-Military Decoration" but considered a personal decoration by the Coast Guard. Originally a "table" (non-wearable) medal then worn with a 2" wide ribbon

27. Aerial Achievement Medal

Service: Air Force

Instituted: 1988

Criteria: Sustained meritorious achievement while participating in aerial flight

Devices: Bronze, silver oak leaf cluster (28, 32)

Notes: Considered on a par with the Air Medal but more likely to be awarded for peacetime actions

Plate 2. U.S. Personal Decorations - Sheet 3

28. Joint Service Commendation Medal

29. Army Commendation Medal

30. Navy Commendation Medal

31. Air Force Commendation Medal

32. Coast Guard Commendation Medal

33. Joint Service Achievement Medal

34. Army Achievement Medal

35. Navy Achievement Medal

36. Air Force Achievement Medal

37. Coast Guard Achievement Medal

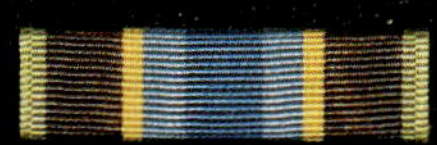

38. Commandant's Letter Of Commendation Ribbon

39. Combat Action Ribbon

United States Personal Decorations (cont'd)

28. Joint Service Commendation Medal

Service: All Services (by Secretary of Defense)

Instituted: 1963

Criteria: Meritorious service or achievement while assigned to a Joint Activity
Devices: Army/Air Force/ Navy/Marine Corps: bronze letter "V" (for valor) (17), bronze, silver oak leaf cluster (29, 33); Coast Guard: bronze letter "V" (for valor), gold, silver star (65, 69)
Notes: Coast Guard uses gold star device since the oak leaf cluster may not be worn on its uniform

29. Army Commendation Medal

Service: Army

Instituted: 1945 (retroactive to 1941)

Criteria: Heroism, meritorious achievement or meritorious service

Devices: Bronze letter "V" (for valor) (17), bronze, silver oak leaf cluster (28, 32)

Notes: Originally a ribbon-only award then designated "Army Commendation Ribbon with Metal Pendant". Redesignated: "Army Commendation Medal" in 1960

30. Navy Commendation Medal

Service: Navy/Marine Corps

Instituted: 1944 (retroactive to 1941)

Criteria: Heroic or meritorious achievement or service

Devices: Bronze letter "V" (for valor) (17), gold, silver star (66, 70)

Notes: Originally a ribbon-only award then designated "Navy Commendation Ribbon with Metal Pendant". Redesignated: "Navy Commendation Medal" in 1960

31. Air Force Commendation Medal

Service: Air Force

Instituted: 1958

Criteria: Outstanding achievement or meritorious service rendered on behalf of the United States Air Force

Devices: Bronze, silver oak leaf cluster (28, 32)

32. Coast Guard Commendation Medal

Service: Coast Guard

Instituted: 1947

Criteria: 1. Heroic or meritorious achievement or service. 2. Meritorious service resulting in unusual or outstanding achievement

Devices: Silver letter "O" (14), bronze letter "V" (for valor) (17), gold, silver star (66, 70)

Notes: Originally "Commendation Ribbon with Metal Pendant". Redesignated: "Coast Guard Commendation Medal" in 1959

33. Joint Service Achievement Medal

Service: All Services (by Secretary of Defense)

Instituted: 1983

Criteria: Meritorious service or achievement while serving with a Joint Activity

Devices: Army/Air Force/ Navy/Marine Corps: bronze, silver oak leaf cluster (29, 33); Coast Guard: gold, silver star (65, 69)

Notes: Coast Guard uses gold star device since the oak leaf cluster may not be worn on its uniform

34. Army Achievement Medal

Service: Army

Instituted: 1981

Criteria: Meritorious service or achievement while serving in a non-combat area

Devices: Bronze, silver oak leaf cluster (28, 32)

35. Navy Achievement Medal

Service: Navy/Marine Corps

Instituted: 1961

Criteria: Meritorious service or achievement in a combat or noncombat situation based on sustained performance of a superlative nature
Devices: Bronze letter "V" (for valor) (17), gold, silver star (66, 70)
Notes: Originally a ribbon-only award: "Secretary of the Navy Commendation for Achievement Award with Ribbon". Changed to present form in 1967

36. Air Force Achievement Medal

Service: Air Force

Instituted: 1980

Criteria: Outstanding achievement or meritorious service not warranting award of the Air Force Commendation Medal

Devices: Bronze, silver oak leaf cluster (28, 32)

37. Coast Guard Achievement Medal

Service: Coast Guard

Instituted: 1964

Criteria: Professional and/or leadership achievement in a combat or non-combat situation

Devices: Silver letter "O" (14), bronze letter "V" (for valor) (17), gold, silver star (66, 70)
Notes: Originally a ribbon-only award. Present configuration adopted in 1968

38. Commandant's Letter of Commendation Ribbon

Service: Coast Guard

Instituted: 1979

Criteria: Receipt of a letter of commendation for an act or service resulting in unusual and/or outstanding achievement

Devices: Silver letter "O" (14), gold, silver star (66, 70)

39. Combat Action Ribbon

Service: Navy/Marine Corps

Instituted: 1969

Criteria: Active participation in ground or air combat during specifically listed military operations

Devices: Gold, silver star (66, 70)

Plate 3. U.S. Special Service, Good Conduct & Reserve Awards

40. Prisoner Of War Medal

41. Combat Readiness Medal

42. Army Good Conduct Medal

43. Navy Good Conduct Medal

44. Marine Corps Good Conduct Medal

45. Air Force Good Conduct Medal

46. Coast Guard Good Conduct Medal

47. Reserve Good Conduct Medal

48. Army Reserve Components Achievment Medal

49. Naval Reserve Meritorious Service Medal

50. Air Reserve Forces Meritorious Service Medal

51. Selected Marine Corps Reserve Medal

52. Fleet Marine Force Ribbon

53. Outstanding Airman of the Year Ribbon

54. Air Force Recognition Ribbon

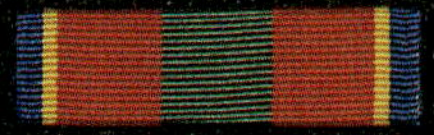

55. Navy Reserve Special Commendation Ribbon (Obsolete)

Special Service, Good Conduct & Reserve Meritorious Awards

40. Prisoner of War Medal

Service: All Services

Instituted: 1989

Criteria: Awarded to any member of the U.S. Armed Forces taken prisoner during any armed conflict dating from World War I

Devices: Bronze, silver star (49, 59)

41. Combat Readiness Medal

Service: Air Force

Instituted: 1964

Criteria: Awarded for specific periods of qualifying service in a combat or mission-ready status

Devices: Bronze, silver oak leaf cluster (27, 31)

42. Army Good Conduct Medal

Service: Army

Instituted: 1941

Criteria: Exemplary conduct, efficiency and fidelity during three years of active enlisted service with the U.S. Army (1 year during wartime)

Devices: Bronze, silver, gold knotted bar (4)

43. Navy Good Conduct Medal

Service: Navy

Instituted: 1888

Criteria: Outstanding performance and conduct during 4 years of continuous active enlisted service in the U.S. Navy

Devices: Bronze, silver star (52, 60)

Notes: Earlier ribbon was a brighter shade of red

44. Marine Corps Good Conduct Medal

Service: Marine Corps

Instituted: 1896

Criteria: Outstanding performance and conduct during 3 years of continuous active enlisted service in the U.S. Marine Corps

Devices: Bronze, silver star (52, 60)

Notes: Earlier ribbon was 1 1/4" wide

45. Air Force Good Conduct Medal

Service: Air Force

Instituted: 1953

Criteria: Exemplary conduct, efficiency and fidelity during three years of active enlisted service with the U.S. Air Force

Devices: Bronze, silver oak leaf cluster (28, 32)

46. Coast Guard Good Conduct Medal

Service: Coast Guard

Instituted: 1921

Criteria: Outstanding proficiency, leadership and conduct during 3 continuous years of active enlisted Coast Guard service

Devices: Bronze, silver star (55, 61)

Notes: Earlier ribbon was 1 1/2" wide

47. Coast Guard Reserve Good Conduct Medal

Service: Coast Guard

Instituted: 1963

Criteria: Outstanding proficiency, leadership and conduct during 3 years of enlisted service in the Coast Guard Reserve

Devices: Bronze, silver star (55, 61), bronze letter "M" (12A)

Notes: Originally a ribbon-only award- "Coast Guard Reserve Meritorious Service Ribbon"

48. Army Reserve Components Achievement Medal

Service: Army

Instituted: 1971

Criteria: Exemplary conduct, efficiency and fidelity during 4 years of enlisted service with the U.S. Army Reserve or National Guard

Devices: Bronze, silver oak leaf cluster (28, 32), bronze letter "M" (12A)

49. Naval Reserve Meritorious Service Medal

Service: Navy

Instituted: 1964

Criteria: Outstanding performance and conduct during 4 years of enlisted service in the Naval Reserve

Devices: Bronze, silver star (52, 60), bronze letter "M" (12A)

Notes: Originally a ribbon-only award.

50. Air Reserve Forces Meritorious Service Medal

Service: Air Force

Instituted: 1964

Criteria: Exemplary behavior, efficiency and fidelity during three years of active enlisted service with the Air Force Reserve

Devices: Bronze, silver oak leaf cluster (28, 32), bronze letter "M" (12A)

51. Selected Marine Corps Reserve Medal

Service: Marine Corps

Instituted: 1939

Criteria: Outstanding performance and conduct during 4 years of enlisted service in the Marine Corps Selected Reserve

Devices: Bronze, silver star (52, 60), bronze letter "M" (12A)

Notes: Formerly: "Organized Marine Corps Reserve Medal"

52. Fleet Marine Force Ribbon

Service: Navy

Instituted: 1984

Criteria: Active participation by professionally skilled Navy personnel with the Fleet Marine Force

Devices: None

53. Outstanding Airman of the Year Ribbon

Service: Air Force

Instituted: 1968

Criteria: Awarded to airmen for selection to the "12 Outstanding Airmen of the Year" Competition Program

Devices: Bronze, silver oak leaf cluster (27, 31), bronze star (50)

54. Air Force Recognition Ribbon

Service: Air Force

Instituted: 1980

Criteria: Awarded to individual recipients of Air Force-level special trophies and awards

Devices: Bronze, silver oak leaf cluster (27, 31)

55. Navy Reserve Special Commendation Ribbon (obsolete)

Service: Navy/Marine Corps

Instituted: 1946

Criteria: Awarded to Reserve Officers with 4 years of successful command and a total Reserve service of 10 years

Devices: None

Plate 4. U.S. Service Medals - Sheet 1

56. Navy Expeditionary Medal

57. Marine Corps Expeditionary Medal

58. China Service Medal

59. American Defense Service Medal

60. Women's Army Corps Service Medal

61. American Campaign Medal

62. Asiatic-Pacific Campaign Medal

63. European-African-Middle Eastern Campaign Medal

64. World War II Victory Medal

65. U. S. Antarctic Expedition Medal

66. Army of Occupation Medal

67. Navy Occupation Medal

56. Navy Expeditionary Medal

Service: Navy

Instituted: 1936

Dates: 1936 to Present

Criteria: Landings on foreign territory and operations against armed opposition for which no specific campaign medal has been authorized

Devices: Silver letter "W" (19) (denotes bar below), Bronze, silver star (52, 60)

Bars: "Wake Island"

57. Marine Corps Expeditionary Medal

Service: Marine Corps

Instituted: 1919

Dates: 1919 to Present

Criteria: Landings on foreign territory and operations against armed opposition for which no specific campaign medal has been authorized

Devices: Silver letter "W" (19) (denotes bar below), bronze, silver star (52, 60)

Notes: Originally a "ribbon-only" award

Bars: "Wake Island"

58. China Service Medal

Service: Navy/Marine Corps/Coast Guard

Instituted: 1940

Dates: 1937-39, 1945-57

Criteria: Service ashore in China or on-board naval vessels during either of the above periods

Devices: Bronze star (54)

Notes: Medal was reinstituted in 1947 for extended service during dates shown above

59. American Defense Service Medal

Service: All Services

Instituted: 1941

Dates: 1939-41

Criteria: Army: 12 months of active duty service during the above period; Naval Services: Any active duty service

Devices: All Services: bronze star (48) (denotes bars below); All Naval Services: bronze letter "A" (8) (not worn with bronze star [device no.48] above)
Bars: Army/Air Force: "Foreign Service", All Naval Services: "Base", "Fleet"

60. Women's Army Corps Service Medal

Service: Army

Instituted: 1943

Dates: 1941-46

Criteria: Service with both the Women's Army Auxiliary Corps and Women's Army Corps during the above period

Devices: None

Notes: Only U.S. award authorized for women only.

61. American Campaign Medal

Service: All Services

Instituted: 1942

Dates: 1941-46

Criteria: Service outside the U.S. in the American theater for 30 days, or within the continental U.S. for one year.

Devices: All Services: bronze, silver star (46, 58); Navy: bronze Marine Corps device (20); Navy/Marine Corps: silver star (72) (obsolete)

62. Asiatic-Pacific Campaign Medal

Service: All Services

Instituted: 1942

Dates: 1941-46

Criteria: Service in the Asiatic-Pacific theater for 30 day or receipt of any combat decoration

Devices: All Services: bronze, silver star (46, 58); Army/Air Force: bronze arrowhead (2); Navy: bronze Marine Corps device (20); Navy/Marine Corps: silver star (72) (obsolete)

63. European-African-Middle Eastern Campaign Medal

Service: All Services

Instituted: 1942

Dates: 1941-45

Criteria: Service in the European-African-Middle Eastern theater for 30 days or receipt of any combat decoration
Devices: All Services: bronze, silver star (46, 58); Army/Air Force: bronze arrowhead (2); Navy: bronze Marine Corps device (20); Navy/Marine Corps: silver star (72) (obsolete)

64. World War II Victory Medal

Service: All Services

Instituted: 1945

Dates: 1941-46

Criteria: Awarded for service in the U.S. Armed Forces during the above period

Devices: None

65. U.S. Antarctic Expedition Medal

Service: Navy/Coast Guard

Instituted: 1945

Dates: 1939-41

Criteria: Awarded in gold, silver and bronze to members of the U.S. Antarctic Expedition of 1939-41

Devices: None

66. Army of Occupation Medal

Service: Army/Air Force

Instituted: 1946

Dates: 1945-55 (Berlin: 1945-90)

Criteria: 30 consecutive days of service in occupied territories of former enemies during above period

Devices: Gold airplane (1)
Bars: "Germany", "Japan" (no associated ribbon device)

67. Navy Occupation Medal

Service: Navy/Marine Corps/Coast Guard

Instituted: 1948

Dates: 1945-55 (Berlin: 1945-90)

Criteria: 30 consecutive days of service in occupied territories of former enemies during above period

Devices: Gold airplane (1)
Bars: "Europe", "Asia" (no associated ribbon device)

Plate 4. U.S. Service Medals - Sheet 2

68. Medal for Humane Action

69. National Defense Service Medal

70. Korean Service Medal

71. Antarctica Service Medal

72. Arctic Service Medal

73. Armed Forces Expeditionary Medal

74. Vietnam Service Medal

75. Southwest Asia Service Medal

76. Humanitarian Service Medal

77. Outstanding Volunteer Service Medal

78. Armed Forces Reserve Medal

79. Naval Reserve Medal (Obsolete)

United States Service Medals (cont'd)

68. Medal for Humane Action Service: All Services Instituted: 1949 Dates: 1948-49 Criteria: 120 consecutive days of service participating in the Berlin Airlift or in support thereof Devices: None	69. National Defense Service Medal Service: All Services Instituted: 1953 Dates: 1950-54, 1961-74, 1990 to Present Criteria: Any honorable active duty service during any of the above periods Devices: All Services: bronze star (44); Army: bronze oak leaf cluster (30) (obsolete) Notes: Reinstituted in 1966 and 1991 for Vietnam and Southwest Asia (Gulf War) actions respectively	70. Korean Service Medal Service: All Services Instituted: 1950 Dates: 1950-54 Criteria: Participation in military operations within the Korean area during the above period Devices: All Services: bronze, silver star (46, 58); Army/Air Force: bronze arrowhead (2); Navy: bronze Marine Corps device (20)	71. Antarctica Service Medal Service: All Services Instituted: 1960 Dates: 1946 to Present Criteria: 30 calendar days of service on the Antarctic Continent Devices: Bronze, gold, silver disks (5) (denote bars below) Bars: "Wintered Over" in bronze, gold, silver
72. Arctic Service Medal Service: Coast Guard Instituted: 1976 Dates: 1946 to Present Criteria: Awarded for 21 days of service on vessels operating in polar waters north of the Arctic Circle Devices: For all deployments after 1 January 1989: bronze, silver star (55, 61)	73. Armed Forces Expeditionary Medal Service: All Services Instituted: 1961 Dates: 1958 to Present Criteria: Participation in military operations not covered by specific war medal Devices: All Services: bronze, silver star (46, 58); Army: bronze arrowhead (2); Navy: bronze Marine Corps device (20) Notes: Authorized for service in Vietnam until establishment of Vietnam Service Medal	74. Vietnam Service Medal Service: All Services Instituted: 1965 Dates: 1965-73 Criteria: Service in Vietnam, Laos, Cambodia or Thailand during the above period Devices: All Services: bronze, silver star (46, 58); Army: bronze arrowhead (2); Navy: bronze Marine Corps device (20)	75. Southwest Asia Service Medal Service: All Services Instituted: 1992 Dates: 1991 to Present Criteria: Active participation in, or support of, Operations Desert Shield and/or Desert Storm Devices: All Services: bronze star (46); Navy: bronze Marine Corps device (20) Notes: Terminal date of service not established as of the date of this writing
76. Humanitarian Service Medal Service: All Services Instituted: 1977 Dates: 1975 to Present Criteria: Direct participation in specific operations of a humanitarian nature Devices: All Services: bronze, silver star (49, 59); Army/Air Force/Navy Marine Corps: bronze numeral (22) (obsolete)	77. Outstanding Volunteer Service Medal Service: All Services Instituted: 1993 Dates: 1993 to Present Criteria: Awarded for outstanding and sustained voluntary service to the civilian community Devices: bronze, silver star (49, 59)	78. Armed Forces Reserve Medal Service: All Services Instituted: 1950 Dates: 1949 to Present Criteria: 10 years of honorable service in any reserve component of the United States Armed Forces Reserve Devices: Bronze hourglass (7), bronze letter "M" (12A)	79. Naval Reserve Medal (obsolete) Service: Navy Instituted: 1938 Dates: 1938-58 Criteria: 10 years of honorable service in the U.S. Naval Reserve Devices: Bronze star (52) Notes: Replaced by the Armed Forces Reserve Medal (No. 78 at left). Some earlier versions had deep red ("plum") ribbon.

Plate 5. U.S. Marksmanship Awards

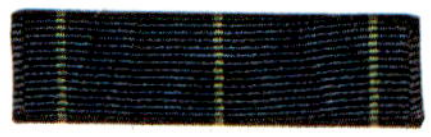

82. Navy Rifle Marksmanship Ribbon

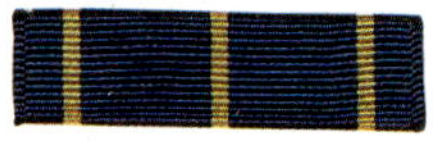

84. Navy Distinguished Marksman Ribbon (0)

83. Navy Pistol Marksmanship Ribbon

85. Navy Distinguished Pistol Shot Ribbon (0)

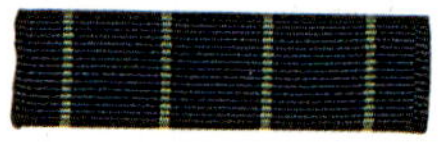

86. Navy Distinguished Marksman and Pistol Shot Ribbon (Obsolete)

80. Navy Expert Rifleman Medal

81. Navy Expert Pistol Shot Medal

87. Air Force Small Arms Expert Marksmanship Ribbon

87a. Air Force Small Arms Expert Marksmanship Ribbon (With Device)

88. Coast Guard Expert Rifleman Medal

89. Coast Guard Expert Pistol Shot

90. Coast Guard Rifle Marksmanship Ribbon

91. Coast Guard Pistol Marksmanship Ribbon

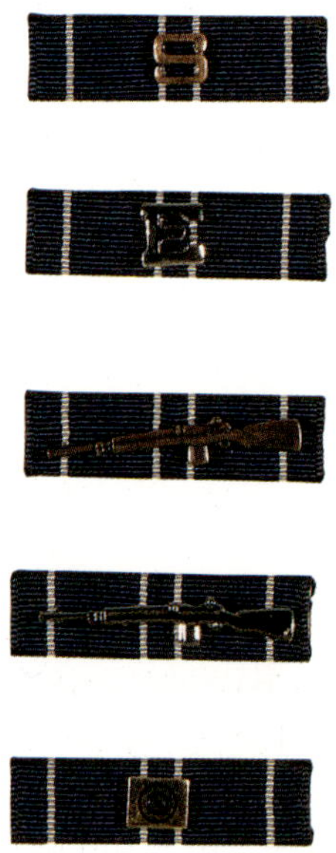

90a. Coast Guard Rifle Marksmanship Ribbon (With Devices)

91a. Coast Guard Pistol Marksmanship Ribbon (With Devices)

United States Marksmanship Awards

80. Navy Expert Rifleman Medal

Service: Navy

Criteria: Attainment of the minimum qualifying score for the expert level during prescribed shooting exercises

Devices: None on medal (but see item 82)

81. Navy Expert Pistol Shot Medal

Service: Navy

Criteria: Attainment of the minimum qualifying score for the expert level during prescribed shooting exercises

Devices: None on medal (but see item 83)

82. Navy Rifle Marksmanship Ribbon

83. Navy Pistol Marksmanship Ribbon

Service: Navy
Criteria: Attainment of the minimum qualifying score during prescribed shooting exercises
Devices: Bronze, silver letter "E" (9, 10), bronze letter "S" (15)

84. Navy Distinguished Marksman Ribbon (obsolete)

85. Navy Distinguished Pistol Shot Ribbon (obsolete)

Service: Navy
Criteria: Attainment of the minimum qualifying score during prescribed shooting exercises
Devices: None

86. Navy Distinguished Marksman and Pistol Shot Ribbon (obsolete)

Service: Navy

Criteria: Attainment of the minimum qualifying score during prescribed shooting exercises
Devices: None

87. Small Arms Expert Marksmanship Ribbon

Service: Air Force

Instituted: 1962
Criteria: Qualification as expert with either the M-16 rifle or standard Air Force issue handgun
Devices: Bronze star (51)

87a. Small Arms Expert Marksmanship Ribbon

Service: Air Force

Shown with 3/16" diameter bronze star

88. Coast Guard Expert Rifleman Medal

Service: Coast Guard

Criteria: Attainment of the minimum qualifying score for the expert level during prescribed shooting exercises
Devices: None on medal (but see item 90)

89. Coast Guard Expert Pistol Shot Medal

Service: Coast Guard

Criteria: Attainment of the minimum qualifying score for the expert level during prescribed shooting exercises
Devices: None on medal (but see item 91)

90. Coast Guard Rifle Marksmanship Ribbon

Service: Coast Guard

Criteria: Attainment of the minimum qualifying score during prescribed shooting exercises

Devices: Bronze, silver letter "E" (9, 10), silver letter "S" (16), bronze, silver rifle (40, 41), gold rifle target (77)

91. Coast Guard Pistol Marksmanship Ribbon

Service: Coast Guard

Criteria: Attainment of the minimum qualifying score during prescribed shooting exercises

Devices: Bronze, silver letter "E" (9, 10), silver letter "S" (16), bronze, silver rifle (40, 41), gold rifle target (77)

90a Coast Guard Rifle Marksmanship Ribbon

91a Coast Guard Pistol Marksmanship Ribbon

Shown With Applicable Ribbon Devices

90a		91a
1a. Silver Letter "S"		1b. Silver Letter "S"
2a. Silver Letter "E"	Bronze Letter "E" (Obsolete)	2b. Silver Letter "E"
3a. Bronze Rifle		3b. Bronze Pistol
4a. Silver Rifle		4b. Silver Pistol
5a. Gold Rifle Target		5b. Gold Pistol Target

Note: The target device on ribbon 5a. above should be mounted on ribbon 5b. and vice versa.

92. Croix de Guerre (France)

93. Croix de Guerre (Belgium)

94. Philippine Defense Medal

95. Philippine Liberation Medal

96.Philippine Independence Medal

97. Republic Of Vietnam Gallantry Cross

98. Republic Of Vietnam Armed Forces Honor Medal

99. Republic Of Vietnam Staff Service Medal

100. Republic Of Vietnam Civil Actions Service Medal

101. Republic of Vietnam Campaign Medal

102. United Nations Service Medal (Korea)

103. United Nations Medal (Observer Medal)

104. Multinational Force and Observers Medal

105. Inter-American Defense Board Medal

106. Saudi Arabian Medal for the Liberation of Kuwait

Foreign Decorations & Non-U.S. Service Awards

92. Croix de Guerre

Country: France

Instituted: 1941

Criteria: Individual feats of arms as recognized by mention in dispatches

Devices: Bronze palm similar to (36), bronze, silver, gold stars similar to (73) through (75) denote level of award and additional awards

93. Croix de Guerre

Country: Belgium

Instituted: 1915

Criteria: Acts of courage on the field of battle as recognized by mention in dispatches

Devices: Silver palms or circular bronze or silver devices bearing the Royal Lion

Notes: The ribbon shown was adopted during World War II (1939-45)

94. Defense Medal/ Ribbon

Country: Republic of the Philippines

Instituted: 1945 (Army: 1948)

Criteria: Service in defense of the Philippines between 8 December 1941 and 15 June 1942

Devices: Bronze star (47)

Notes: Only the ribbon may be worn on the U.S. military uniform

95. Liberation Medal/ Ribbon

Country: Republic of the Philippines

Instituted: 1945 (Army: 1948)

Criteria: Service in the liberation of the Philippines between 17 October 1944 and 3 September 1945

Devices: Bronze star (47)

Notes: Only the ribbon may be worn on the U.S. military uniform

96. Independence Medal/Ribbon

Country: Republic of the Philippines

Instituted: 1946 (Army: 1948)

Criteria: Receipt of both the Philippine Defense and Liberation Medals/Ribbons. Originally presented to those present for duty in the Philippines on 4 July 1946

Devices: None

Notes: Only the ribbon may be worn on U.S. military uniform

97. Gallantry Cross

Country: Republic of Vietnam

Instituted: 1950

Criteria: Deeds of valor and acts of courage/heroism while fighting the enemy

Devices: Bronze palm similar to (36), bronze, silver, gold stars similar to (73) through (75) denote level of award and additional awards

98. Armed Forces Honor Medal

Country: Republic of Vietnam

Instituted: 1953

Criteria: For outstanding contributions to the training and development of RVN Armed Forces

Devices: None

Notes: 1st Class for officers is shown; the 2nd Class ribbon does not have the yellow edge stripes

99. Staff Service Medal

Country: Republic of Vietnam

Instituted: 1964

Criteria: For outstanding initiative and devotion to their staff duties

Devices: None

Notes: 1st Class for officers is shown; the 2nd Class ribbon has blue edges

100. Civil Actions Service Medal

Country: Republic of Vietnam

Instituted: 1964

Criteria: For outstanding achievements in the field of civic actions

Devices: None

Notes: 1st Class for officers is shown; the 2nd Class ribbon has no center red stripes

101. Republic of Vietnam Campaign Medal

Service: All Services

Instituted: 1966

Criteria: 6 months service in the Republic of Vietnam between 1965 and 1973 or if wounded, captured or killed in action during the above period

Devices: Silver date bar (3)

102. United Nations Service Medal (Korea)

Service: All Services

Instituted: 1951

Criteria: Service on behalf of the United Nations in Korea between 27 June 1950 and 27 July 1954

Devices: None

Notes: Above date denotes when award was authorized for wear by U.S. military personnel

103. United Nations Medal (Observer Medal)

Service: All Services

Instituted: 1964

Criteria: 6 months service with any of the following U.N. operations: UNTSO, UNOGIL, UNMOGIP or UNSFH

Devices: None

Notes: Above date denotes when award was authorized for wear by U.S. military personnel

104. Multinational Force and Observers Medal

Service: All Services

Instituted: 1982

Criteria: 6 months service with the Multinational Force & Observers peacekeeping force in the Sinai Desert

Devices: Bronze numeral (23)

Notes: Above date denotes when award was authorized for wear by U.S. military personnel

105. Inter-American Defense Board Medal

Service: All Services

Instituted: 1982

Criteria: Service with the Inter-American Defense Board

Devices: Gold star (67)

Notes: Above date denotes when award was authorized for wear by U.S. military personnel

106. Saudi Arabian Medal for the Liberation of Kuwait

Service: All Services

Instituted: 1992

Criteria: Participation in, or support of, Operations Desert Shield and/or Desert Storm (1991-92)

Devices: Gold palm tree device (37)

Notes: Only foreign service award for the Gulf War authorized for wear by U.S. military personnel

Plate 7. U.S. Awards Having No Medal Awards ("Ribbons-Only")

107. Navy Sea Service Deployment Ribbon

108. Navy Arctic Service Ribbon

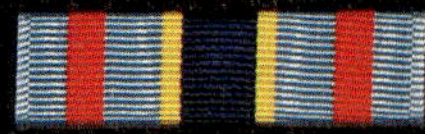

109. Naval Reserve Sea Service Ribbon

110. Navy and Marine Corps Overseas Service Ribbon

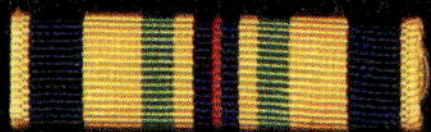

111. Navy Recruiting Service Ribbon

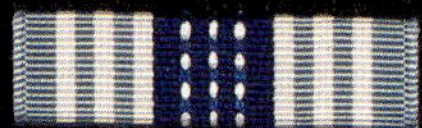

112. Air Force Overseas Service Ribbon (Short Tour)

113. Air Force Overseas Service Ribbon (Long Tour)

114. Coast Guard Special Operations Service Ribbon

115. Coast Guard Sea Service Ribbon

116. Coast Guard Restricted Duty Ribbon

117. Coast Guard Basic Training Honor Graduate Ribbon

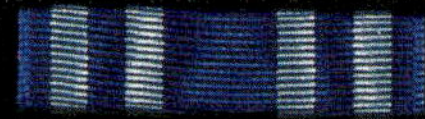

118. Air Force Longevity Service Award

119. Marine Corps Reserve Ribbon

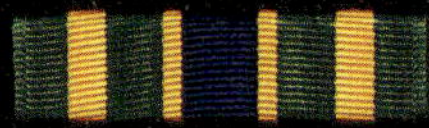

120. Army N.C.O. Professional Development Ribbon

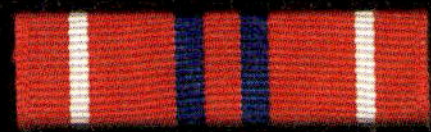

121. Air Force N.C.O. Professional Military Education Graduate Ribbon

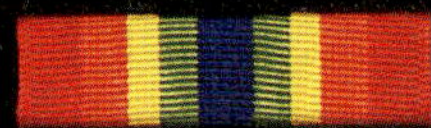

122. Army Service Ribbon

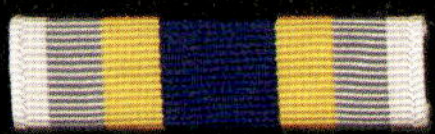

123. Air Force Basic Military Training Honor Graduate

124. Army Overseas Service Ribbon

125. Army Reserve Components Overseas Training Ribbon

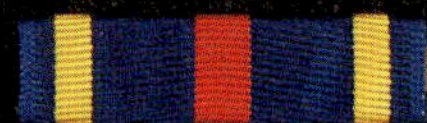

126. Air Force Training Ribbon

U.S. Awards Having No Medals ("Ribbons-Only")

107. Navy Sea Service Deployment Ribbon

Service: Navy/Marine Corps (Inst: 1981)

Criteria: 12 months active duty on deployed vessels operating away from their home port for extended periods

Devices: Bronze, silver star (52, 60)

108. Navy Arctic Service Ribbon

Service: Navy/Marine Corps (Inst: 1986)

Criteria: 28 days of service on naval vessels operating above the Arctic Circle

Devices: None

109. Naval Reserve Sea Service Ribbon

Service: Navy (Inst: 1986)

Criteria: 24 months of cumulative service embarked on Naval Reserve vessels or an embarked Reserve unit

Devices: Bronze, silver star (52, 60)

110. Navy and Marine Corps Overseas Service Ribbon

Service: Navy/Marine Corps (Inst: 1986)

Criteria: 12 months consecutive or accumulated duty at an overseas shore base duty station

Devices: Bronze, silver star (52, 60)

111. Navy Recruiting Service Ribbon

Service: Navy (Inst: 1989)

Criteria: Successful completion of 3 consecutive years of recruiting duty

Devices: Bronze, silver star (52, 60)

112. Overseas Service Ribbon (Short Tour)

Service: Air Force (Inst: 1980)

Criteria: Successful completion of an overseas tour designated as "short term" by appropriate authority

Devices: Bronze, silver oak leaf cluster (28, 32)

113. Overseas Service Ribbon (Long Tour)

Service: Air Force (Inst: 1980)

Criteria: Successful completion of an overseas tour designated as "long term" by appropriate authority

Devices: Bronze, silver oak leaf cluster (28, 32)

114. Special Operations Service Ribbon

Service: Coast Guard (Inst: 1987)

Criteria: Participation in a Coast Guard special non-combat operation not recognized by another service award

Devices: Bronze, silver star (55, 61)

115. Coast Guard Sea Service Ribbon

Service: Coast Guard (Inst: 1984)

Criteria: Satisfactory completion of a minimum of 12 months of cumulative sea duty

Devices: Bronze, silver star (55, 61)

116. Restricted Duty Ribbon

Service: Coast Guard (Inst: 1984)

Criteria: Successful completion of a tour of duty at remote shore stations (LORAN stations, light ships, etc.) without family

Devices: Bronze, silver star (55, 61)

117. Coast Guard Basic Training Honor Graduate Ribbon

Service: Coast Guard (Inst: 1984)

Criteria: Successful attainment of the top 3 percent of the class during Coast Guard recruit training

Devices: None

118. Air Force Longevity Service Award

Service: Air Force (Inst: 1957)

Criteria: Successful completion of an aggregate total of four years of honorable active service

Devices: Bronze, silver oak leaf cluster (28, 32)

119. Marine Corps Reserve Ribbon

Service: Marine Corps (Inst: 1945)

Criteria: Successful completion of 10 years of honorable service in any class of the Marine Corps Reserve

Devices: Bronze star (52)

120. N.C.O. Professional Development Ribbon

Service: Army (Inst: 1981)

Criteria: Successful completion of designated NCO professional development courses

Devices: Bronze numeral (24)

121. N.C.O. Professional Military Education Graduate Ribbon

Service: Air Force (Inst: 1962)

Criteria: Successful completion of a certified NCO professional military education school

Devices: Bronze, silver oak leaf cluster (27, 31)

122. Army Service Ribbon

Service: Army (Inst: 1981)

Criteria: Successful completion of initial entry training

Devices: None

123. Basic Military Training Honor Graduate Ribbon

Service: Air Force (Inst: 1976)

Criteria: Demonstration of excellence in all academic and military training phases of basic Air Force entry training

Devices: None

124. Army Overseas Service Ribbon

Service: Army (Inst: 1981)

Criteria: Successful completion of normal overseas tours not recognized by any other service award

Devices: Bronze numeral (25)

125. Army Reserve Components Overseas Training Ribbon

Service: Army (Inst: 1984)

Criteria: Successful completion of annual training or active duty training for 10 consecutive duty days on foreign soil

Devices: Bronze numeral (25)

126. Air Force Training Ribbon

Service: Air Force (Inst: 1980)

Criteria: Successful completion of an Air Force accession training program

Devices: Bronze, silver oak leaf cluster (27, 31)

Plate 8. U.S. and Foreign Unit Awards

127. Army Presidential Unit Citation

128. Navy Presidential Unit Citation

129. Air Force Presidential Unit Citation

130. Joint Meritorious Unit Award

131. Army Valorous Unit Award

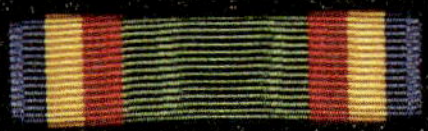
132. Navy Unit Commendation

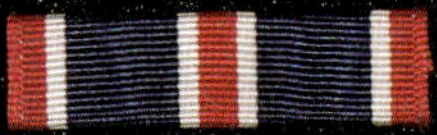
133. Air Force Outstanding Unit Award

134. Coast Guard Unit Commendation

135. Army Meritorious Unit Commendation

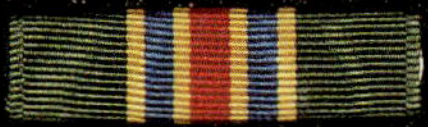
136. Navy Meritorious Unit Commendation

137. Air Force Organizational Excellence Award

138. Coast Guard Meritorious Unit Commendation

139. Army Superior Unit Award

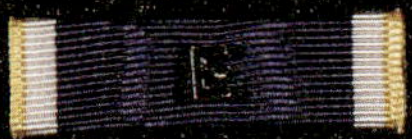
140. Navy "E" Ribbon

141. Coast Guard "E" Ribbon

142. Coast Guard Bicentennial Unit Commendation

143. Philippine Presidential Unit Citation

144. Korean Presidential Unit Citation

145. Vietnam Presidential Unit Citation

146. Republic of Vietnam Gallantry Cross Unit Citation

147. Republic of Vietnam Civil Actions Unit Citation

United States and Foreign Unit Awards

127. Army Presidential Unit Citation

Service: Army (Inst: 1942)

Criteria: Awarded to U.S. Army units for extraordinary heroism in action against an armed enemy

Devices: Bronze, silver oak leaf cluster (28, 32)
Notes: Original designation: Distinguished Unit Citation. Redesignated to present name in 1966

128. Navy Presidential Unit Citation

Service: Navy/Marine Corps/ Coast Guard (Inst: 1942)

Criteria: Awarded to Navy/ Marine Corps units for extraordinary heroism in action against an armed enemy

Devices: Gold globe (6), gold letter "N" (13), blue star (43), bronze, silver star (52, 60)

129. Air Force Presidential Unit Citation

Service: Air Force (Inst: 1957)

Criteria: Awarded to Air Force units for extraordinary heroism in action against an armed enemy

Devices: Bronze, silver oak leaf cluster (28, 32)
Notes: Original designation: Distinguished Unit Citation. Redesignated to present name in 1966

130. Joint Meritorious Unit Award

Service: All Services (Inst: 1982)

Criteria: Awarded to Joint Service units for meritorious achievement or service in combat or extreme circumstances
Devices: Army/Air Force/ Navy/Marine Corps: Bronze, silver oak leaf cluster (29, 33); Coast Guard: bronze, silver star (56, 62)

131. Army Valorous Unit Award

Service: Army (Inst: 1963)

Criteria: Awarded to U.S. Army units for outstanding heroism in armed combat against an opposing armed force

Devices: Bronze, silver oak leaf cluster (28, 32)

132. Navy Unit Commendation

Service: Navy/Marine Corps (Inst: 1944)

Criteria: Awarded to units Navy/Marine Corps for outstanding heroism in action or extremely meritorious service

Devices: Bronze, silver star (52, 60)

133. Air Force Outstanding Unit Award

Service: Air Force (Inst: 1954)

Criteria: Awarded to U.S. Air Force units for exceptionally meritorious achievement or meritorious service

Devices: Bronze letter "V" (18), bronze, silver oak leaf cluster (28, 32)

134. Coast Guard Unit Commendation

Service: Coast Guard (Inst: 1963)

Criteria: Awarded to U.S. Coast Guard units for valorous or extremely meritorious service not involving combat

Devices: Silver letter "O" (14), gold, silver star (64, 68)

135. Army Meritorious Unit Commendation

Service: Army (Inst: 1944)

Criteria: Awarded to U.S. Army units for exceptionally meritorious conduct in the performance of outstanding service
Devices: Bronze, silver oak leaf cluster (28, 32)
Notes: Originally a golden wreath worn on the lower sleeve. Authorized in its present form in 1961

136. Navy Meritorious Unit Commendation

Service: Navy/Marine Corps (Inst: 1967)

Criteria: Awarded to Navy/ Marine Corps units for valorous actions or meritorious achievement (combat or noncombat)

Devices: Bronze, silver star (52, 60)

137. Air Force Organizational Excellence Award

Service: Air Force (Inst: 1969)

Criteria: Same as Outstanding Unit Award (see no.133 above) but awarded to unique unnumbered organizations performing staff functions

Devices: Bronze letter "V" (18), bronze, silver oak leaf cluster (28, 32)

138. Coast Guard Meritorious Unit Commendation

Service: Coast Guard (Inst: 1973)

Criteria: Awarded to U.S. Coast Guard units for valorous or meritorious achievement (combat or noncombat)

Devices: Silver letter "O" (14), gold, silver star (64, 68)

139. Army Superior Unit Award

Service: Army (Inst: 1983)

Criteria: Awarded to U.S. Army units for meritorious performance in difficult and challenging peacetime missions
Devices: Bronze, silver oak leaf cluster (28, 32)

140. Navy "E" Ribbon

Service: Navy/Marine Corps (Inst: 1976)

Criteria: Awarded to ships or squadrons which have won battle efficiency competitions

Devices: Silver letter "E" (11), wreathed silver letter "E" (12)

141. Coast Guard "E" Ribbon

Service: Coast Guard (Inst: 1990)

Criteria: Awarded to U.S. Coast Guard ships and cutters which earn the overall operational readiness efficiency award
Devices: Gold, silver star (64, 68)

142. Coast Guard Bicentennial Unit Commendation

Service: Coast Guard (Inst: 1990)

Criteria: Awarded to all Coast Guard personnel serving satisfactorily at any time between 4 June 1989 and 4 June 1990
Devices: None

143. Philippine Presidential Unit Citation

Service: All Services (Inst: 1948)

Criteria: Awarded to units of the U.S. Armed Forces for service in the war against Japan and/or for 1970 and 1972 disaster relief

Devices: All Services (except Army) Bronze star (45)

144. Korean Presidential Unit Citation

Service: All Services (Inst: 1951)

Criteria: Awarded to certain units of the U.S. Armed Forces for services rendered during the Korean War

Devices: None

145. Vietnam Presidential Unit Citation

Service: Army/Navy/Marine Corps/Coast Guard (Inst: 1954)

Criteria: Awarded to certain units of the U.S. Armed Forces for humanitarian service in the evacuation of civilians from North and Central Vietnam

Devices: None

146. Republic of Vietnam Gallantry Cross Unit Citation

Service: All Services (Inst: 1966)

Criteria: Awarded to certain units of the U.S. Armed Forces for valorous combat achievement during the Vietnam War, 1 March 1961 to 28 March 1974
Devices: Bronze palm, (34, 36), gold, silver, bronze star (73, 74, 75)

147. Republic of Vietnam Civil Actions Unit Citation

Service: All Services (Inst: 1966)

Criteria: Awarded to certain units of the U.S. Armed Forces for meritorious service during the Vietnam War , 1 March 1961 to 28 March 1974

Devices: Bronze palm (35)

Plate 9. Correct Manner of Wear-Ribbons of the U.S. Army

UNIT AWARDS
RIGHT BREAST

7. ARMED FORCES RIBBON DISPLAYS

CORRECT MANNER OF WEAR- RIBBONS OF THE U.S. ARMY

LEFT BREAST	Medal of Honor	Distinguished Service Cross	Defense Distinguished Service Medal
Army Distinguished Service Medal	Silver Star	Defense Superior Service Medal	Legion of Merit
Distinguished Flying Cross	Soldier's Medal	Bronze Star Medal	Purple Heart
Defense Meritorious Service Medal	Meritorious Service Medal	Air Medal	Joint Service Commendation Medal
Army Commendation Medal	Joint Service Achievement Medal	Army Achievement Medal	Prisoner of War Medal
Army Good Conduct Medal	Reserve Components Achievement Medal	American Defense Service Medal	Women's Army Corps Service Medal
American Campaign Medal	Asiatic-Pacific Campaign Medal	Eur.-African-Middle Eastern Campaign	World War II Victory Medal
Army of Occupation Medal	Medal for Humane Action	National Defense Service Medal	Korean Service Medal
Antarctica Service Medal	Armed Forces Expeditionary Medal	Vietnam Service Medal	Southwest Asia Service Medal
Humanitarian Service Medal	Outstanding Volunteer Service Medal	Armed Forces Reserve Medal	NCO Professional Development Ribbon
Army Service Ribbon	Overseas Service Ribbon	Reserve Comp.Over-seas Training Ribbon	Philippine Defense Ribbon
Philippine Liberation Ribbon	Philippine Independence Ribbon	United Nations Service Medal	Inter-American Defense Board Medal
United Nations Medal	Multinational Force and Observers Medal	Republic of Vietnam Campaign Medal	Kuwait Liberation Medal (Saudi Arabia)

RIGHT BREAST	Army Presidential Unit Citation	
Joint Meritorious Unit Award	Valorous Unit Award	Army Meritorious Unit Commendation
Army Superior Unit Award	Philippine Presidential Unit Citation	Korean Presidential Unit Citation
Vietnam Presidential Unit Citation	Vietnam Gallantry Cross Unit Citation	Vietnam Civil Act-ions Unit Citation

te 10. Correct Manner of Wear-Ribbons of the U.S. Navy

SEE PAGE 48 FOR RIGHT BREAST DISPLAY ON FULL DRESS UNIFORM

CORRECT MANNER OF WEAR- RIBBONS OF THE U.S. NAVY

	Medal of Honor	Navy Cross	
Defense Distinguished Service Medal	Navy Distinguished Service Medal	Silver Star	Defense Superior Service Medal
Legion of Merit	Distinguished Flying Cross	Navy & Marine Corps Medal	Bronze Star
Purple Heart Medal	Defense Meritorious Service Medal	Meritorious Service Medal	Air Medal
Joint Service Commendation Medal	Navy Commendation Medal	Joint Service Achievement Medal	Navy Achievement Medal
Combat Action Ribbon	Navy Presidential Unit Citation	Joint Meritorious Unit Award	Navy Unit Commendation
Navy Meritorious Unit Commendation	Navy "E" Ribbon	Prisoner of War Medal	Navy Good Conduct Medal
Reserve Special Commendat'n Ribbon	Naval Reserve Meritor-ious Service Medal	Fleet Marine Force Ribbon	Navy Expeditionary Medal
China Service Medal	American Defense Service Medal	American Campaign Medal	Eur.-African-Middle Eastern Campaign
Asiatic-Pacific Campaign Medal	World War II Victory Medal	U.S. Antarctic Expedition Medal	Navy Occupation Service Medal
Medal for Humane Action	National Defense Service Medal	Korean Service Medal	Antarctica Service Medal
Armed Forces Expeditionary Medal	Vietnam Service Medal	Southwest Asia Service Medal	Humanitarian Service Medal
Outstanding Volunteer Service Medal	Sea Service Deployment Ribbon	Arctic Service Ribbon	Naval Reserve Sea Service Ribbon
Navy & M/Corps Over-seas Service Ribbon	Navy Recruiting Service Ribbon	Armed Forces Reserve Medal	Navy Reserve Medal
Foreign Decoration	Philippine President-ial Unit Citation	Korean Presidential Unit Citation	Vietnam Presidential Unit Citation
Vietnam Gallantry Cross Unit Citation	Vietnam Civil Actions Unit Citation	Philippine Defense Ribbon	Philippine Liberation Ribbon
Philippine Independence Ribbon	United Nations Service Medal	United Nations Medal	Multinational Force and Observers Medal
Inter-American Defense Board Medal	Republic of Vietnam Campaign Medal	Kuwait Liberation Medal (Saudi Arabia)	Distinguished Marksman Badge
Distinguished Pistol Shot Badge	Dist. Marksman and Pistol Shot Badge	Rifle Marksmanship Ribbon	Pistol Marksmanship Ribbon

NOTE: Per Navy regulations, no row may contain more than three (3) ribbons. The above display is arranged solely to conserve space on the page.

Plate 11. Correct Manner of Wear-Ribbons of the U.S. Marine Corps

SEE PAGE 48 FOR RIGHT BREAST DISPLAY ON FULL DRESS UNIFORM

CORRECT MANNER OF WEAR- RIBBONS OF THE U.S. MARINE CORPS

Medal of Honor	Navy Cross	Defense Distinguished Service Medal	Navy Distinguished Service Medal
Silver Star	Defense Superior Service Medal	Legion of Merit	Distinguished Flying Cross
Navy & Marine Corps Medal	Bronze Star Medal	Purple Heart	Defense Meritorious Service Medal
Meritorious Service Medal	Air Medal	Joint Service Commendation Medal	Navy Commendation Medal
Joint Service Achievement Medal	Navy Achievement Medal	Combat Action Ribbon	Navy Presidential Unit Citation
Joint Meritorious Unit Award	Navy Unit Commendation	Navy Meritorious Unit Commendation	Navy "E" Ribbon
Prisoner of War Medal	Marine Corps Good Conduct Medal	Selected Marine Corps Reserve Medal	Marine Corps Expeditionary Medal
China Service Medal	American Defense Service Medal	American Campaign Medal	Eur.-African-Middle Eastern Campaign
Asiatic-Pacific Campaign Medal	World War II Victory Medal	Navy Occupation Service Medal	Medal for Humane Action
National Defense Service Medal	Korean Service Medal	Antarctica Service Medal	Armed Forces Expeditionary Medal
Vietnam Service Medal	Southwest Asia Service Medal	Humanitarian Service Medal	Outstanding Volunteer Service Medal
Sea Service Deployment Ribbon	Arctic Service Ribbon	Navy & M/Corps Over-seas Service Ribbon	Armed Forces Reserve Medal
Marine Corps Reserve Ribbon	Foreign Decoration	Philippine President-ial Unit Citation	Korean Presidential Unit Citation
Vietnam Presidential Unit Citation	Vietnam Gallantry Cross Unit Citation	Vietnam Civil Actions Unit Citation	Philippine Defense Ribbon
Philippine Liberation Ribbon	Philippine Independence Ribbon	United Nations Service Medal	United Nations Medal
Multinational Force and Observers Medal	Inter-American Defense Board Medal	Republic of Vietnam Campaign Medal	Kuwait Liberation Medal (Saudi Arabia)

2. Correct Manner of Wear-Ribbons of the U.S. Air Force

CORRECT MANNER OF WEAR- RIBBONS OF THE U.S. AIR FORCE

	Medal of Honor	Air Force Cross	
Defense Distinguished Service Medal	Air Force Dist. Service Medal	Silver Star	Defense Superior Service Medal
Legion of Merit	Distinguished Flying Cross	Airman's Medal	Bronze Star Medal
Purple Heart	Defense Meritorious Service Medal	Meritorious Service Medal	Air Medal
Aerial Achievement Medal	Joint Service Commendation Medal	Air Force Commendation Medal	Joint Service Achievement Medal
Air Force Achievement Medal	Air Force President-ial Unit Citation	Joint Meritorious Unit Award	Outstanding Unit Award
Organizational Excellence Award	Prisoner of War Medal	Combat Readiness Medal	Air Force Good Conduct Medal
Air Reserve Forces Mer.Service Medal	Outstanding Airman of the Year Ribbon	Air Force Recognition Ribbon	American Defense Service Medal
Women's Army Corps Service Medal	American Campaign Medal*	Eur.-African-Middle Eastern Campaign*	Asiatic-Pacific Campaign Medal*
World War II Victory Medal	Army of Occupation Medal	Medal for Humane Action	National Defense Service Medal
Korean Service Medal	Antarctica Service Medal	Armed Forces Expeditionary Medal	Vietnam Service Medal
Southwest Asia Service Medal	Humanitarian Service Medal	Outstanding Volunteer Service Medal	Overseas Service Ribbon- Short Tour
Overseas Service Ribbon- Long Tour	Longevity Service Award Ribbon	Armed Forces Reserve Medal	NCO Prof.Military Educat'n Grad.Ribbon
Basic Mil.Training Honor Grad.Ribbon	Small Arms Expert Marksmanship Ribbon	Training Ribbon	Philippine Defense Ribbon
Philippine Liberation Ribbon	Philippine Independence Ribbon	Philippine President-ial Unit Citation	Korean Presidential Unit Citation
Vietnam Gallantry Cross Unit Citation	Vietnam Civil Actions Unit Citation	United Nations Service Medal	United Nations Medal
Multinational Force and Observers Medal	Inter-American Defense Board Medal	Republic of Vietnam Campaign Medal	Kuwait Liberation Medal (Saudi Arabia)

<u>NOTE:</u> 1. * These items are worn in the order earned

Plate 13. Correct Manner of Wear-Ribbons of the U.S. Coast Guard

Correct Order for U.S. Merchant Marine

CORRECT MANNER OF WEAR- RIBBONS OF THE U.S. COAST GUARD

Medal of Honor	Navy Cross	Defense Distinguished Service Medal	Transportation Dist. Service Medal
Coast Guard Dist. Service Medal	Silver Star	D.O.T. Sec'y Award for Outstanding Achvment	Defense Superior Service Medal
Legion of Merit	Distinguished Flying Cross	Coast Guard Medal	Gold Lifesaving Medal
Bronze Star Medal	Purple Heart	Defense Meritorious Service Medal	Meritorious Service Medal
Air Medal	Silver Lifesaving Medal	D.O.T. Sec'y Award for Meritorious Achvment	Joint Service Commendation Medal
Coast Guard Commendation Medal	D.O.T. Award for Superior Achievement	Joint Service Achievement Medal	Coast Guard Achievement Medal
Commandant's Letter of Commendation Ribn	Combat Action Ribbon	Navy Presidential Unit Citation	Joint Meritorious Unit Award
Coast Guard Unit Commendation	C.G. Meritorious Unit Commendation	C.G. Meritorious Team Commendation	Coast Guard "E" Ribbon
C.G. Bicentennial Unit Commendation	Prisoner of War Medal	Coast Guard Good Conduct Medal	Coast Guard Reserve Good Conduct Medal
Navy Expeditionary Medal	China Service Medal	American Defense Service Medal	American Campaign Medal
Eur.-African-Middle Eastern Campaign	Asiatic-Pacific Campaign Medal	World War II Victory Medal	U.S. Antarctic Expedition Medal
Navy Occupation Service Medal	Medal for Humane Action	National Defense Service Medal	Korean Service Medal
Antarctica Service Medal	Arctic Service Medal	Armed Forces Expeditionary Medal	Vietnam Service Medal
Southwest Asia Service Medal	Humanitarian Service Medal	Outstanding Volunteer Service Medal	Special Operations Service Ribbon
Coast Guard Sea Service Ribbon	Restricted Duty Ribbon	Basic Training Honor Graduate Ribbon	Armed Forces Reserve Medal
Philippine Presidential Unit Citation	Korean Presidential Unit Citation	Vietnam Presidential Unit Citation	Vietnam Gallantry Cross Unit Citation
Vietnam Civil Actions Unit Citation	Philippine Defense Ribbon	Philippine Liberation Ribbon	Philippine Independence Ribbon
United Nations Service Medal	United Nations Medal	Multinational Force and Observers Medal	Inter-American Defense Board Medal
Republic of Vietnam Campaign Medal	Kuwait Liberation Medal (Saudi Arabia)	Rifle Marksmanship Ribbon	Pistol Marksmanship Ribbon

NOTE: Per Coast Guard regulations, no row may contain more than three (3) ribbons. The above display is arranged solely to conserve space on the page.

CORRECT MANNER OF WEAR- RIBBONS OF THE U.S. MERCHANT MARINE

	Distinguished Service Medal		
Meritorious Service Medal	Mariner's Medal	Gallant Ship Citation Bar	
Merchant Marine Combat Bar	Prisoner-of-War Medal	Merchant Marine Defense Medal	
Atlantic War Zone Medal	Pacific War Zone Medal	Mediterranean- Mid-East War Zone Medal	
World War II Victory Medal	Korean Service Medal	Vietnam Service Medal	
Merchant Marine Expeditionary Medal	Philippine Defense Ribbon	Philippine Liberation Ribbon	40th Anniversary of World War II (USSR)

Note: Some references show the Mariner's Medal and the Gallant Ship Citation Bar reversed in precedence

8. RIGHT BREAST DISPLAYS/FULL DRESS

The three Naval Services prescribe the wear of "ribbon-only" awards on the right breast of the full dress uniform when full-size medals are worn. The resulting displays are depicted on the following pages:

CORRECT MANNER OF WEAR- RIBBONS OF THE U.S. NAVY (RIGHT BREAST DISPLAY ON FULL DRESS UNIFORM)

	Navy Presidential Unit Citation	Combat Action Ribbon
Navy Meritorious Unit Commendation	Navy Unit Commendation	Joint Meritorious Unit Award
Fleet Marine Force Ribbon	Reserve Special Commendat'n Ribbon	Navy "E" Ribbon
Naval Reserve Sea Service Ribbon	Arctic Service Ribbon	Sea Service Deployment Ribbon
Philippine Presidential Unit Citation	Navy Recruiting Service Ribbon	Navy & M/Corps Overseas Service Ribbon
Vietnam Gallantry Cross Unit Citation	Vietnam Presidential Unit Citation	Korean Presidential Unit Citation
Philippine Liberation Ribbon	Philippine Defense Ribbon	Vietnam Civil Actions Unit Citation
Philippine Independence Ribbon	Pistol Marksmanship Ribbon	Rifle Marksmanship Ribbon

CORRECT MANNER OF WEAR- RIBBONS OF THE U.S. MARINE CORPS (RIGHT BREAST DISPLAY ON FULL DRESS UNIFORMS)

Combat Action Ribbon	Navy Presidential Unit Citation	Joint Meritorious Unit Award
Navy Unit Commendation	Navy Meritorious Unit Commendation	Navy "E" Ribbon
Sea Service Deployment Ribbon	Arctic Service Ribbon	Navy & M/Corps Overseas Service Ribbon
Marine Corps Reserve Ribbon	Philippine Presidential Unit Citation	Korean Presidential Unit Citation
Vietnam Presidential Unit Citation	Vietnam Gallantry Cross Unit Citation	Vietnam Civil Actions Unit Citation
Philippine Defense Ribbon	Philippine Liberation Ribbon	Philippine Independence Ribbon

CORRECT MANNER OF WEAR- RIBBONS OF THE U.S. COAST GUARD (RIGHT BREAST DISPLAY ON FULL DRESS UNIFORMS)

Combat Action Ribbon	Commandant's Letter of Commendation Rbn	
Coast Guard Unit Commendation	Joint Meritorious Unit Award	Navy Presidential Unit Citation
Coast Guard "E" Ribbon	C.G. Meritorious Team Commendation	C.G. Meritorious Unit Commendation
Coast Guard Sea Service Ribbon	Special Operations Service Ribbon	C.G. Bicentennial Unit Commendation
Philippine Presidential Unit Citation	Basic Training Honor Graduate Ribbon	Restricted Duty Ribbon
Vietnam Gallantry Cross Unit Citation	Vietnam Presidential Unit Citation	Korean Presidential Unit Citation
Philippine Liberation Ribbon	Philippine Defense Ribbon	Vietnam Civil Actions Unit Citation
Pistol Marksmanship Ribbon	Rifle Marksmanship Ribbon	Philippine Independence Ribbon

U.S. MERCHANT MARINE MEDALS AND DECORATIONS

To you who answered the call of your country and served in its Merchant Marine ... **President Harry S. Truman**

Distinguished Service Medal
The Merchant Marine's Highest Award

Under authority of Public law 100-324, the Maritime Administration shall award this medal to seamen who distinguished themselves by outstanding conduct or service beyond the line of duty.

Meritorious Service Medal

Under authority of Public Law 100-324, the Maritime Administration shall award this medal to seamen for conduct or service of a meritorious nature.

Gallant Ship Plaque

Gallant Ship Citation Ribbon

Awarded to officers and seamen who served on a ship which, at the time of service, was cited for gallantry by the Maritime Administration. The bronze plaque is awarded to the ship.

Mariner's Medal
(World War II)

Awarded to a seaman who, while serving on a ship from December 7, 1941, and July 25, 1947, was wounded or suffered physical injury as a result of an act of an enemy of the United States.

Merchant Marine Defense Medal
(World War II)

Awarded for service in the U.S. Merchant Marine prior to Pearl Harbor. It may be worn by all merchant seamen who served as members of the crews of U.S. merchant ships from September 8, 1939, and December 7, 1941.

Atlantic War Zone Medal
(World War II)

Awarded for service in the Atlantic War Zone, including the North Atlantic, South Atlantic, Gulf of Mexico, Carribean, Barents Sea, and the Greenland Sea, during the period December 7, 1941, to November 8, 1945.

Mediterranean-Middle East War Zone Medal
(World War II)

Awarded for service in the zone including the Mediterranean Sea, Red Sea, Arabian Sea, and Indian Ocean west of 80 degrees east longitude, during the period December 7, 1941, to November 8, 1945.

Pacific War Zone Medal
(World War II)

Awarded for service in the Pacific War Zone, including the North Pacific, South Pacific, and the Indian Ocean east of 80 degrees east longitude, during the period December 7, 1941, to March 2, 1946.

Victory Medal
(World War II)

Awarded to members of the crews of ships who served for 30 days or more during the period December 7, 1941, to September 3, 1945.

Merchant Marine Combat Bar
(World War II)

Awarded to merchant seamen who served on a ship which at the same time of such service was attacked or damaged by an instrumentality of war from December 7, 1941, and July 25, 1947. A star is attached if the seaman was forced to abandon ship. For each additional abandonment a star is added.

Merchant Marine Emblem
(World War II)

The emblem is an identifying insigne that was issued to active merchant seamen for service from December 7, 1941, to July 25, 1947.

Honorable Service Button
(World War II)

Awarded to members of the crews of ships who served for 30 days during the period December 7, 1941, to September 3, 1945.

Korean Service Medal

Awarded for service in the merchant marine from June 30, 1950, and September 30, 1953 in waters adjacent to Korea.

Vietnam Service Medal

Awarded for service in the merchant marine from July 4, 1965, and August 15, 1973 in waters adjacent to Vietnam.

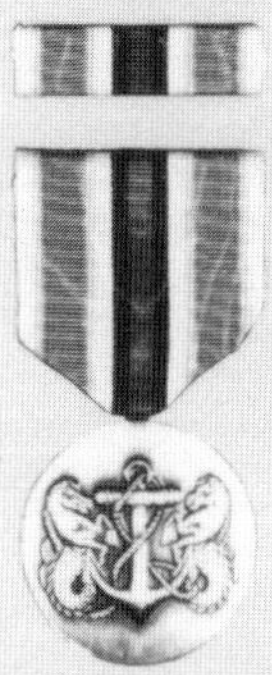

Merchant Marine Expeditionary Award

Awarded to American merchant seamen who serve on U.S. flag ships in support of operations involving American and allied military forces as authorized by the Maritime Administration.

DEPARTMENT OF DEFENSE AND FOREIGN GOVERNMENTS RECOGNITION

Prisoner of War Medal
(U.S. Department of Defense)

Awarded to World War II merchant marine veterans held prisoners of war during the period December 7, 1941, to August 15, 1945. The medal recognizes the special service prisoners of war gave to their country and the suffering and anguish they endured while incarcerated.

Soviet Commemorative Medal

Awarded to merchant marine veterans who participated in convoys to Murmansk during World War II.

Phillippine Defense Ribbon

Awarded to members of crews of ships who served in Phillippine waters for not less than 30 days from December 8, 1941, to June 15, 1942.

Phillippine Liberation Ribbon

Awarded to members of crews of ships who served in Phillippine waters for not less than 30 days from October 17, 1944, to September 3, 1945.

Applications for or inquiries relating to merchant marine medals and decorations should be directed to U.S. Department of Transportation, Maritime Administration, Office of Maritime Labor and Training, Washington, DC 20590.

U.S. Department of Transportation
Maritime Administration

10. ATTACHMENTS and DEVICES

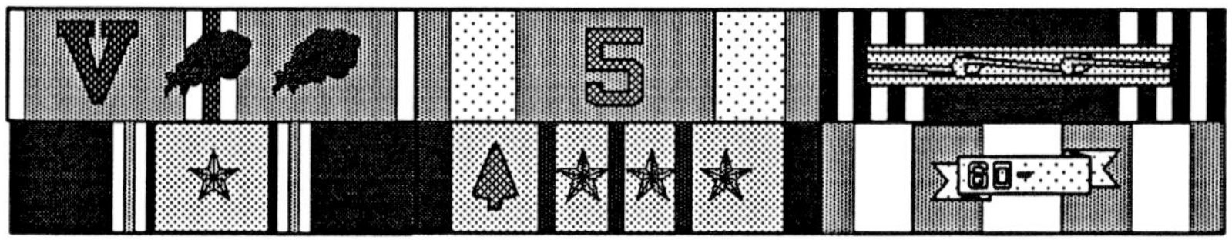

Looking back from the perspective of the late 20th century, it is apparent that early in the history of the U.S. awards program, little attention was paid to the possibility that a medal could be bestowed upon an individual more than once. This was to cause some embarrassment when five individuals (three Army and two Marine Corps) won second awards of the Medal of Honor in the span of years between the Civil War and World War I.

In contrast, the British Empire had recognized this need as far back as 1856 when the Victoria Cross was instituted. The original Royal Warrant authorized the use of an ornate bar affixed to the medal's suspension ribbon to represent the second award of the Cross. The bar, however, was not used universally and had to be authorized on an individual basis as each new medal was introduced or many years thereafter. Also to be noted, the custom of wearing a device directly on the ribbon bar to denote an additional award was still many years away, not finding its way into Victoria Cross regulations until 1916.

Although no one in possession of all his faculties would characterize World War I as an Age of Enlightenment, that certainly describes the era from the standpoint of medal and ribbon devices. By the end of the Great War, the use of ribbon attachments was quite widespread throughout the world and the U.S. had instituted its first four ribbon attachments, thus setting the stage for the many such accessories which would follow.

The best known of these, the oak leaf cluster, was established (although not by that name) at the same time that the Army's Distinguished Service Cross and Distinguished Service Medal came into being. The 1918 regulations provided for "..a bar or other suitable device.." for each succeeding deed or act sufficient to justify a subsequent award".

The same act authorized the use of a silver star device, three-sixteenths of an inch in diameter to denote a citation for gallantry in action. Although the directive seemed quite straightforward, it never made clear the actual ribbon to which the star should be affixed. However, the War Department directed that it be used on the appropriate service medal/ribbon. This led to a large number of retroactive awards, some dating back to the Civil War, but of greater significance, to the establishment of the Silver Star Medal as described earlier in this book. As a footnote to this discussion, the U.S. Navy also adopted the small silver star device but only for wear on the ribbon of the World War I Victory Medal after the receipt of a letter of commendation for performance of duty not justifying the award of the Medal of Honor, Navy Cross or Distinguished Service Medal (the only decorations in existence at the time).

For the record, the other two ribbon attachments authorized for use just after the Great War were the 3/16" diameter bronze stars representing the battle clasps to the Victory Medal and the bronze scroll numeral (now obsolete) used on the Marine Corps Expeditionary Ribbon (not a Medal yet!) to indicate the number of additional awards of the ribbon. Note that the Navy did not authorize its 5/16" diameter gold star to denote additional awards of a decoration until the early 1920s.

The great number of decorations and awards created during World War II also resulted in a vast increase in the number of available devices. The most significant of these was the silver device used in a five-for-one swap to eliminate the clutter that resulted from the huge number of decorations being awarded at the time. As an example, an Airman could now display 13 awards of the Air Medal with only four oak leaf clusters, 2 bronze and 2 silver, with the ribbon itself representing one award. The Navy's 5/16" silver star and the universally-used 3/16" silver "battle star" also aided in the war on ribbon clutter.

This is not to say that the device situation today is as clear as crystal. The bare fact is that, exclusive of the Merchant Marine, only 9 ribbons authorized since World War II have **no** device associated with their wear on the uniform. More to the point, there are only four ribbons awarded today that fit this category.

One might bemoan the use of all that hardware on the chest but, given the use of awards as a means of managing today's vastly scaled-down military establishment, it makes some sense. One need only examine the awards of the former Soviet Union to witness the results of having NO means to represent multiple awards of a medal. The great World War II military leaders, in wearing every medal they possessed, virtually covered every available square inch of their tunics with gongs.

Thus, to make some sense of the American system of devices and attachments, the reader is invited to examine the illustrations and tables on the next six pages, noting that the reference number under each device and in the left-hand column of the table is keyed to the earlier text material describing each associated award.

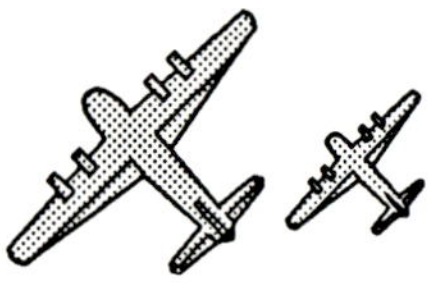

1. Airplane, C-54, Gold

2. Arrowhead, Bronze

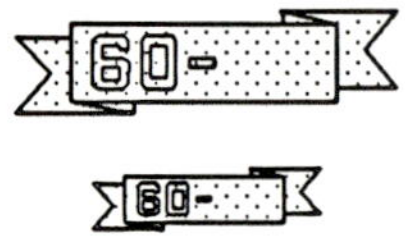

3. Bar, Date Silver

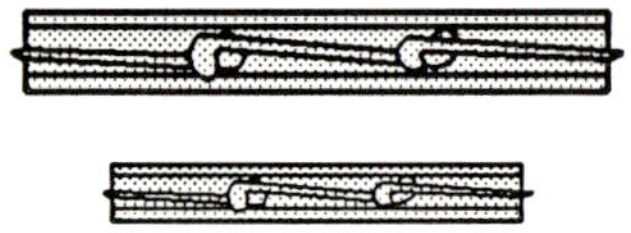

4. Bar, Knotted

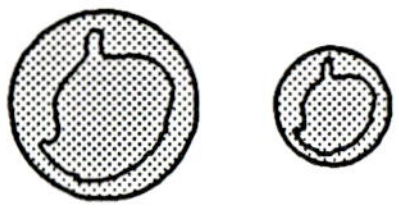

5. Disk, "Wintered Over"

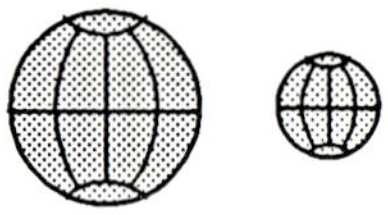

6. Globe, Gold

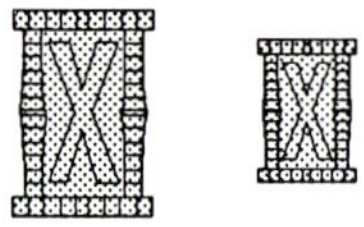

7. Hourglass, Bronze

8. Letter "A" Bronze

9. Letter "E", Bronze

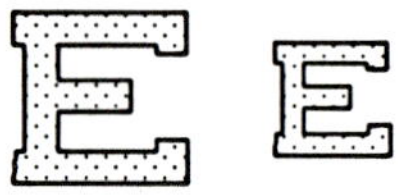

10. Letter "E", Silver

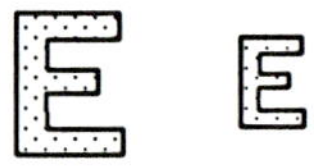

11. Letter "E", Silver

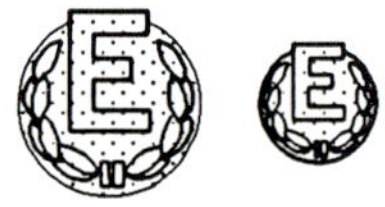

12. Letter "E", Wreathed, Silver

12A. Letter "M", Bronze

13. Letter "N", Gold

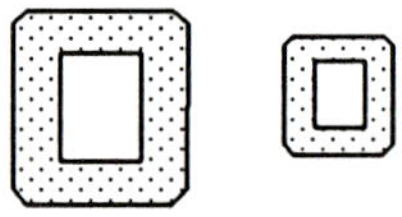

14. Letter "O", Silver

15. Letter "S", Bronze

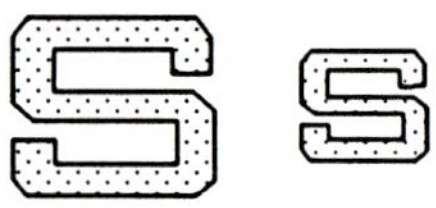

16. Letter "S", Silver

17-18. Letter "V", Bronze

19. Letter "W", Silver

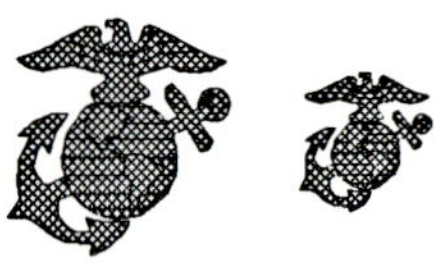

20. Marine Device, Bronze

21-25. Numeral, Bronze

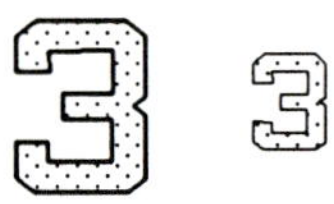

26. Numeral, Gold

<u>Note:</u> All devices are shown both actual size and slightly larger than normal to enhance device details

Plate 16. Attachments/Devices Used on American Ribbons- Sheet 1

27-30. Oak Leaf Cluster, Bronze

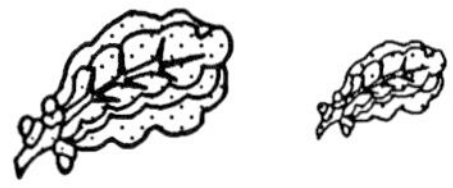

31-33. Oak Leaf Cluster, Silver

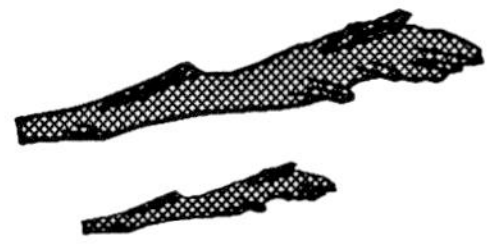

34-35. Palm, Bronze

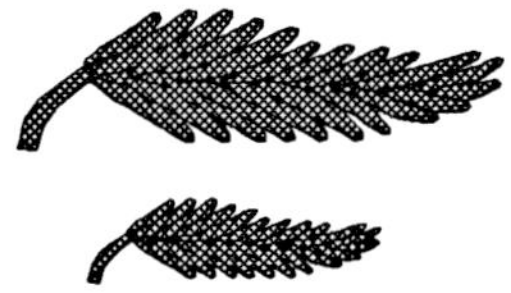

36. Palm, Bronze

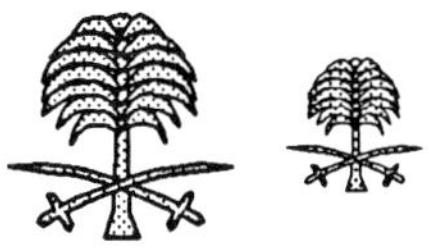

37. Palm Tree & Swords, Gold

38. Pistol, M1911A1, Bronze

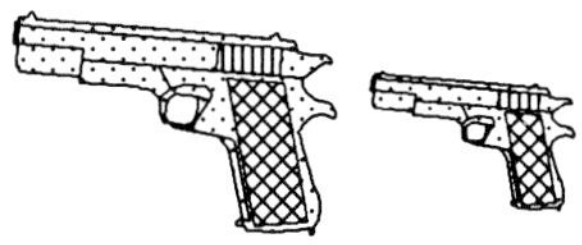

39. Pistol, M1911A1, Silver

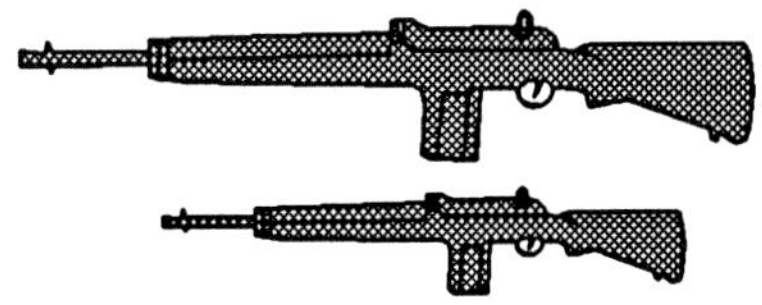

40. Rifle, M14, Bronze

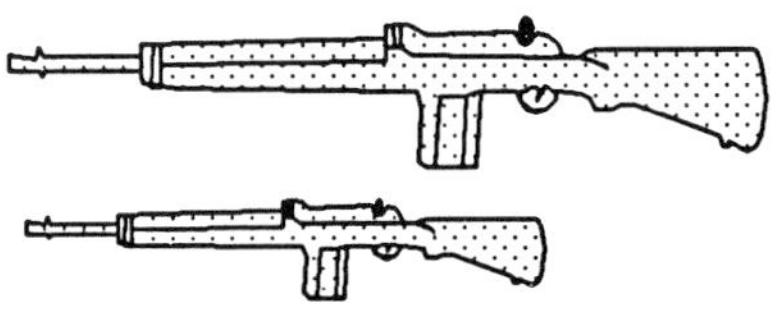

41. Rifle, M14, Silver

42. Seahorse, Silver

43. Star, 3/16", Blue

44-57. Star, 3/16", Bronze

58-63. Star, 3/16", Silver

64-67. Star, 5/16", Gold

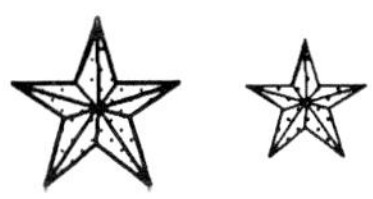

68-72. Star, 5/16", Silver

73. Star, 3/8", Bronze

74. Star, 3/8", Gold

75. Star, 3/8", Silver

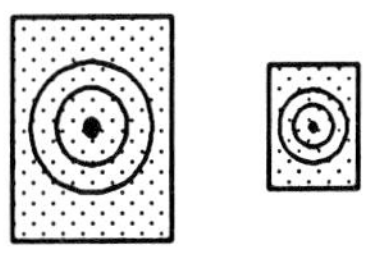

76. Target, Pistol, Gold

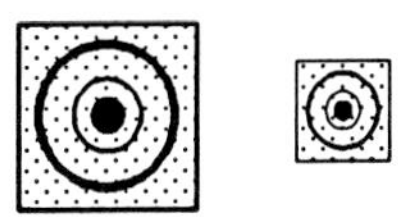

77. Target Rifle, Gold

__Note:__ All devices are shown both actual size and slightly larger than normal to enhance device details

Plate 16. Attachments/Devices Used on American Ribbons- Sheet 2

ATTACHMENTS/DEVICES USED ON AMERICAN RIBBONS

NO	DEVICE	RIBBON USE	DENOTES
1	Airplane, C-54 Gold	ALL SERVICES- World War II Occupation Medal	Berlin Airlift participation
2	Arrowhead, Bronze	ARMY and AIR FORCE- Campaign awards since World War II	Participation in combat glider landing, combat parachute jump or amphibious assault landing
3	Bar, Date, Silver	ALL SERVICES- Republic of Vietnam Campaign Medal	No significance- worn upon initial issue
4	Bar, Knotted:	ARMY- Good Conduct Medal	Additional awards:
	Bronze		Nos. 2 - 5
	Silver		Nos. 6 - 10
	Gold		Nos. 11 - 15
5	Disk, "Wintered-Over"	ALL SERVICES- Antarctica Service Medal	Wintering over on the Antarctic Continent:
	Bronze		1 winters
	Gold		2 winters
	Silver		3 winters
6	Globe, Gold	NAVY- Presidential Unit Citation	Service aboard USS Triton during 1st submerged cruise around the world
7	Hourglass, Bronze	ALL SERVICES- Armed Forces Reserve Medal	Additional award
8	Letter "A", Bronze	NAVY, MARINE CORPS, COAST GUARD- American Defense Service Medal	Atlantic Fleet service prior to World War II
9	Letter "E", Bronze	NAVY and COAST GUARD- Marksmanship awards	Expert- 1st qualification (obsolete)
10	Letter "E", Silver	NAVY and COAST GUARD- Marksmanship awards	Expert qualification
11	" " "	NAVY and MARINE CORPS- Navy "E" Ribbon	One (1) device per award- three (3) maximum
12A	Letter "M", Bronze	ALL SERVICES- Reserve Component medals and Armed Forces Reserve Medal	Mobilization Device for Reservists called to active duty
12	Letter "E", Silver, Wreathed	NAVY and MARINE CORPS- Navy "E" Ribbon	4th (final) award
13	Letter "N", Gold	NAVY- Presidential Unit Citation	Service aboard USS Nautilus during first cruise under the north polar ice cap
14	Letter "O", Silver	COAST GUARD- Decorations and unit awards	Operational Distinguishing Device
15	Letter "S", Bronze	NAVY- Marksmanship awards	Sharpshooter qualification
16	Letter "S", Silver	COAST GUARD- Marksmanship awards	Sharpshooter qualification
17	Letter "V", Bronze	ALL SERVICES- Decorations	Combat Distinguishing Device

ATTACHMENTS/DEVICES USED ON AMERICAN RIBBONS

NO	DEVICE	RIBBON USE	DENOTES
18	Letter "V", Bronze (cont'd)	AIR FORCE- Unit awards	Combat Distinguishing Device
19	Letter "W", Silver	NAVY and MARINE CORPS- Expeditionary Medals	Participation in defense of Wake Island- (1941)
20	Marine Corps Device, Bronze	NAVY and COAST GUARD- Campaign awards since World War II	Combat service by Naval personnel with Marine Corps units
21	Numeral, Block, Bronze	NAVY and MARINE CORPS- Air Medal	Total number of strike/flight awards
22	" " "	ALL SERVICES (except COAST GUARD)- Humanitarian Service Medal	Additional awards (obsolete)
23	" " "	ALL SERVICES- Multinational Force and Observer's Medal	Total number of awards
24	" " "	ARMY- NCO Professional Development Ribbon	Level of professional training attained:
	Basic Ribbon		Primary Level
	Numeral "2"		Basic Level
	Numeral "3"		Advanced Level
	Numeral "4"		Senior Level
	Numeral "5" (obsolete)		Sergeants Major Academy
25	" " "	ARMY- Air Medal and service awards	Total number of awards
26	Numeral, Block, Gold	NAVY and MARINE CORPS- Air Medal	Number of individual awards (obsolete)
27	Oak Leaf Cluster, Bronze	AIR FORCE- Achievement awards	Additional awards
28	" " "	ARMY and AIR FORCE- Decorations, service and unit awards	Additional awards
29	" " "	ALL SERVICES- (except COAST GUARD)- Joint Service decorations and Joint Meritorious Unit Award	Additional awards
30	" " "	ARMY- National Defense Service Medal	Additional award (obsolete)
31	Oak Leaf Cluster, Silver	AIR FORCE- Achievement awards	5 additional awards
32	" " "	ARMY and AIR FORCE- Decorations, service and unit awards	5 additional awards
33	" " "	ALL SERVICES- (except COAST GUARD)- Joint Service decorations and Joint Meritorious Unit Award	5 additional awards
34	Palm, Bronze	ALL SERVICES- (except ARMY) Republic of Vietnam Gallantry Cross Unit Citation	No significance- worn upon initial issue
35	" "	ALL SERVICES- Republic of Vietnam Civil Actions Unit Citation	No significance- worn upon initial issue

ATTACHMENTS/DEVICES USED ON AMERICAN RIBBONS

NO	DEVICE	RIBBON USE	DENOTES
36	Palm, Bronze (cont'd)	ARMY- Republic of Vietnam Gallantry Cross Unit Citation	Level of award ("cited before the Army") and additional awards
37	Palm Tree with Swords, Gold	ALL SERVICES- Kuwait Liberation Medal (Saudi Arabia)	No significance- worn upon initial issue
38	Pistol, M1911A1, Bronze	COAST GUARD- Pistol Marksmanship Ribbon	Recipient of Pistol Shot Excellence in Competition Badge (Bronze)
39	Pistol, M1911A1, Silver	COAST GUARD- Pistol Marksmanship Ribbon	Recipient of Pistol Shot Excellence in Competition Badge (Silver)
40	Rifle, M14, Bronze	COAST GUARD- Rifle Marksmanship Ribbon	Recipient of Rifleman Excellence in Competition Badge (Bronze)
41	Rifle, M14, Silver	COAST GUARD- Rifle Marksmanship Ribbon	Recipient of Rifleman Excellence in Competition Badge (Silver)
42	Seahorse, Silver	MERCHANT MARINE- Gallant Ship Citation Bar	No significance- worn upon initial issue
43	Star, 3/16", Blue	NAVY- Presidential Unit Citation	Additional awards (obsolete)
44	Star, 3/16", Bronze	ALL SERVICES- National Defense Service Medal	Additional awards
45	" " "	ALL SERVICES- (except ARMY)- Philippine Republic Presidential Unit Citation	Additional award
46	" " "	ALL SERVICES- Campaign awards since World War II	Major battle participation (one star per major engagement)
47	" " "	ALL SERVICES- Philippine Defense and Liberation Ribbons	Additional battle honors
48	" " "	ALL SERVICES- American Defense Service Medal	Foreign service prior to World War II
49	" " "	ALL SERVICES- Service awards	Additional awards
50	" " "	AIR FORCE- Outstanding Airman of the Year Ribbon	"One of 12" competition finalist
51	" " "	AIR FORCE- Small Arms Expert Marksmanship Ribbon	Additional weapon qualification
52	" " "	NAVY and MARINE CORPS- Unit and service awards	Additional awards
53	" " "	NAVY and MARINE CORPS- Air Medal	First individual award
54	" " "	NAVY, MARINE CORPS and COAST GUARD- China Service Medal	Additional award (extended service)
55	" " "	COAST GUARD- Service awards	Additional awards

ATTACHMENTS/DEVICES USED ON AMERICAN RIBBONS

NO	DEVICE	RIBBON USE	DENOTES
56	Star, 3/16", Bronze (cont'd)	COAST GUARD- Joint Meritorious Unit Award	Additional award
57	" " "	MERCHANT MARINE- Expeditionary Medal	Additional awards
58	Star, 3/16", Silver	ALL SERVICES- Campaign awards since World War II	Participation in 5 major battles/campaigns
59	" " "	ALL SERVICES- Service awards	5 additional awards
60	" " "	NAVY and MARINE CORPS- Unit and service awards	5 additional awards
61	" " "	COAST GUARD- Service awards	5 additional awards
62	" " "	COAST GUARD- Joint Meritorious Unit Award	5 additional awards
63	" " "	MERCHANT MARINE- Combat Bar	Crew member forced to abandon ship (1 star per sinking)
64	Star, 5/16", Gold	COAST GUARD- Unit awards	Additional awards
65	" " "	COAST GUARD- Joint Service decorations	Additional awards
66	" " "	NAVY, MARINE CORPS and COAST GUARD- Decorations	Additional awards
67	" " "	ALL SERVICES- Inter-American Defense Board Medal	Additional awards
68	Star, 5/16", Silver	COAST GUARD- Unit awards	5 additional awards
69	" " "	COAST GUARD- Joint Service decorations	5 additional awards
70	" " "	NAVY, MARINE CORPS and COAST GUARD- Decorations	5 additional awards
71	" " "	NAVY and MARINE CORPS- Unit awards	5 additional awards (obsolete)
72	" " "	NAVY and MARINE CORPS- Campaign awards	Participation in 5 major battles (obsolete)
73	Star, 3/8", Bronze	ARMY- Republic of Vietnam Gallantry Cross Unit Citation	Level of award (cited before the Regiment) and additional awards
74	Star, 3/8", Gold	ARMY- Republic of Vietnam Gallantry Cross Unit Citation	Level of award (cited before the Corps) and additional awards
75	Star, 3/8", Silver	ARMY- Republic of Vietnam Gallantry Cross Unit Citation	Level of award (cited before the Division) and additional awards
76	Target, Pistol, Gold	COAST GUARD- Pistol Marksmanship Ribbon	Recipient of Distinguished Pistol Shot Badge
77	Target, Pistol, Gold	COAST GUARD- Pistol Marksmanship Ribbon	Recipient of Distinguished Marksman Badge

11. UNDERSTANDING U.S. AWARDS

The evolution of the awards system of the United States may be best characterized as paralleling the American passion for individual freedom. To the casual observer, it might resemble an endless series of unrelated regulations designed to confuse rather than to inform, but upon closer examination, one finds a highly-organized, well-documented system that has been overcomplicated by historical inertia.

When this country won its independence from Great Britain, most British traditions were retained, but all trappings of the old regal system were repudiated. As a result, almost 75 years elapsed between the adoption of the U.S. Constitution and the authorization of our first military award, the Medal of Honor. At that time, however, Congress made no provision for a centralized authority to govern awards that may be established in the future. Whether this was due to persistent fears of an "Imperial Presidency" or purely through oversight is still unclear, but once the War and Navy Departments initiated their own systems of decorations and campaign/service medals, it was evident that our Head of State was not even nominally responsible for the execution of the U.S. awards policy (The President traditionally presents the Medal of Honor but does so in the name of the Congress).

As the number of awards grew, responsibility for the approval and presentation of an award to a recipient became (and remains today) a function of the importance of the proposed award. As in most Armed Services around the world, the immediate field commander is empowered to nominate deserving candidates for an appropriate medal but here the resemblance ends. In the U.S. Army, for example, final award authority can be a Company, Regimental, Brigade or Division Commander providing the award is for a campaign, good conduct, achievement, commendation or meritorious service. Only when the upper strata of the "Pyramid of Honor" are attained (i.e., Bronze Star Medal and above) is the senior level of command (The Chief of Staff, Secretary of the Army or Secretary of Defense) required to act upon such recommendations. The other Services follow this pattern closely, some going even further by delegating the authority to issue a few of the more senior awards to lower echelon commanders during wartime situations.

Having thus created their own historical precedent, the individual Services went on to establish distinct and unique regulations for the display of decorations, medals and service ribbons, a policy that lasted from its Civil War beginnings through the World War II era.

In 1947, when the U.S. Armed Forces were unified into the present Department of Defense, one might have expected a series of orderly and clear-cut directives that would totally reorganize all such awards policies. However, with only a few notable exceptions, (e.g., standardization of the height and width of ribbons plus some award criteria) this has not been the case.

Although Joint Service awards committees do exist, they can only recommend general policies for those items shared by all the Armed Forces, but do NOT have the authority to set standards within the individual Services. As a result, some 74 new awards have been authorized since unification, only 18 of which are common to all the Services and the rules governing the display of ribbons and devices now vary so widely as to require a road map.

1. Order of Precedence

The first area of potential confusion is the order of ribbon wear on the U.S. military uniform. A careful examination of the various awards manuals and uniform regulations shows that three distinct arrangements exist among the five Services (the Navy, Marine Corps and Coast Guard share a common scheme).

Arbitrarily taking the Navy method as a baseline, the various award precedence schemes break down into general categories as follows:

A. U.S. Military Decorations
B. U.S. Unit Awards
C. U.S. Non-Military Decorations

D. U.S. Merchant Marine Decorations
E. Prisoner of War and Good Conduct Medals
F. Campaign, Service and Training Awards
G. U.S. Merchant Marine Service Awards
H. Foreign Military Decorations
I. Foreign Unit Awards
J. Non-U.S. Service Awards
K. Marksmanship Awards

The precedence established by the Army is as follows:

A. U.S. Military Decorations
E. Prisoner of War Medal
C. U.S. Non-Military Decorations
E. Good Conduct Medal
F. Campaign, Service and Training Awards
D. U.S. Merchant Marine Decorations
G. U.S. Merchant Marine Service Awards
H. Foreign Military Decorations
J. Non-U.S. Service Awards

NOTE: All U.S. and foreign unit awards (categories B and I above) are worn on the right breast of the Army uniform.

The Air Force has been left for last owing to its unique set of ribbon rules. Not only is the Air Force arrangement different from those discussed earlier but some of their medals and ribbons, designated as "Achievement Awards", do not fit neatly into the previously-defined categories. The Air Force precedence list is as follows:

A. U.S. Military Decorations
B. U.S. Unit Awards
C. U.S. Non-Military Decorations
D. U.S. Merchant Marine Decorations
E. Prisoner of War Medal
-- Combat Readiness Medal
E. Good Conduct Medal
F. Campaign, Service and Training Awards
K. Marksmanship Awards
-- Air Force Training Ribbon
J. Philippine Service Awards
G. U.S. Merchant Marine Service Awards
H. Foreign Military Decorations
I. Foreign Unit Awards
J. Non-U.S. Service Awards

2. Campaign, Service & Training Awards

In the area of campaign, service and training awards, the Services have again developed different rules and regulations. Air Force award regulations, for example, are roughly chronological, progressing to the present time as follows:

1. Air Reserve Forces Meritorious Service Medal
2. Outstanding Airman of the Year Ribbon
3. Air Force Recognition Ribbon
4. China Service Medal
5. American Defense Service Medal
6. Women's Army Corps Service Medal
7. World War II Campaign Medals (worn in order earned)
8. World War II Victory Medal
9. World War II Occupation Medal
10. Medal for Humane Action
11. National Defense Service Medal
12. Korean Service Medal
13. Antarctica Service Medal
14. Armed Forces Expeditionary Medal
15. Vietnam Service Medal
16. Southwest Asia Service Medal
17. Humanitarian Service Medal
18. Outstanding Volunteer Service Medal
19. Overseas Ribbon (Short Tour)
20. Overseas Ribbon (Long Tour)
21. Longevity Service Award Ribbon
22. Armed Forces Reserve Medal
23. NCO Professional Military Education Graduate Ribbon
24. Basic Military Education Honor Graduate Ribbon

According to applicable Army directives, campaign, service and training awards are worn as follows:

1. Reserve Components Achievement Medal
2. American Defense Service Medal
3. Women's Army Corps Service Medal
4. American Campaign Medal
5. Asiatic-Pacific Campaign Medal
6. European-African-Middle Eastern Campaign Medal
7. World War II Victory Medal
8. Army of Occupation Medal (World War II)
9. Medal for Humane Action
10. National Defense Service Medal

11. Korean Service Medal
12. Antarctica Service Medal
13. Armed Forces Expeditionary Medal
14. Vietnam Service Medal
15. Southwest Asia Service Medal
16. Humanitarian Service Medal
17. Outstanding Volunteer Service Medal
18. Armed Forces Reserve Medal
19. NCO Professional Development Ribbon
20. Army Service Ribbon
21. Overseas Service Ribbon
22. Reserve Components Overseas Training Ribbon

Similarly, the Navy, Marine Corps and Coast Guard have assigned each ribbon a specific slot regardless of the dates of service as follows:

1. Naval Reserve Meritorious Service Medal
2. Selected Marine Corps Reserve Medal
3. Coast Guard Reserve Good Conduct Medal
4. Fleet Marine Force Ribbon (Navy only)
5. Navy/Marine Corps Expeditionary Medals
6. China Service Medal
7. American Defense Service Medal
8. American Campaign Medal
9. European-African-Middle Eastern Campaign Medal
10. Asiatic-Pacific Campaign Medal
11. World War II Victory Medal
12. U.S. Antarctic Expedition Medal
13. Navy Occupation Service Medal (World War II)
14. Medal for Humane Action
15. National Defense Service Medal
16. Korean Service Medal
17. Antarctica Service Medal
18. Arctic Service Medal (Coast Guard only)
19. Armed Forces Expeditionary Medal
20. Vietnam Service Medal
21. Southwest Asia Service Medal
22. Humanitarian Service Medal
23. Outstanding Volunteer Service Medal
24. Sea Service Deployment Ribbon (Navy, Marine Corps only)
25. Arctic Service Ribbon (Navy, Marine Corps only)
26. Naval Reserve Sea Service Ribbon
27. Overseas Service Ribbon (Navy, Marine Corps only)
28. Recruiting Service Ribbon (Navy Only)
29. Special Operations Service Ribbon (Coast Guard only)
30. Sea Service Ribbon (Coast Guard only)
31. Restricted Duty Ribbon (Coast Guard only)
32. Basic Training Honor Graduate Ribbon (Coast Guard only)
33. Armed Forces Reserve Medal
34. Naval Reserve Medal
35. Marine Corps Reserve Ribbon

Although this makes a foolproof method for checking a ribbon display during a full-dress inspection, it has also created the following anomalies:

A. The China Service Medal (Extended) is worn before all World War II service awards in spite of the prescribed dates of service (1945-57).

B. The U.S. Antarctic Expedition Medal is worn after all World War II ribbons although the qualifying dates lie between 1939 and 1941.

C. World War II Area/Campaign Medals are worn in the specific order shown regardless of when earned. This is also true for the Army which seems to favor alphabetical order for the three awards.

D. The Antarctica Service Medal and Coast Guard Arctic Service Medal are worn after the Korean Service Medal although the service may have been performed as early as 1946.

E. The Navy and Marine Corps Expeditionary Medals take precedence over all except the oldest campaign awards with little regard for the dates of service, the most recent being the raids on Libya and the operations in the Persian Gulf prior to the 1990-91 Gulf War.

3. Display of Appurtenances

The next area in which the Services have gone their separate ways is in the prescribed arrangement of the various devices used on the ribbons of decorations and service awards.

Section 10 contains a listing of the devices used on U.S. ribbons, but of particular interest are the following cases:

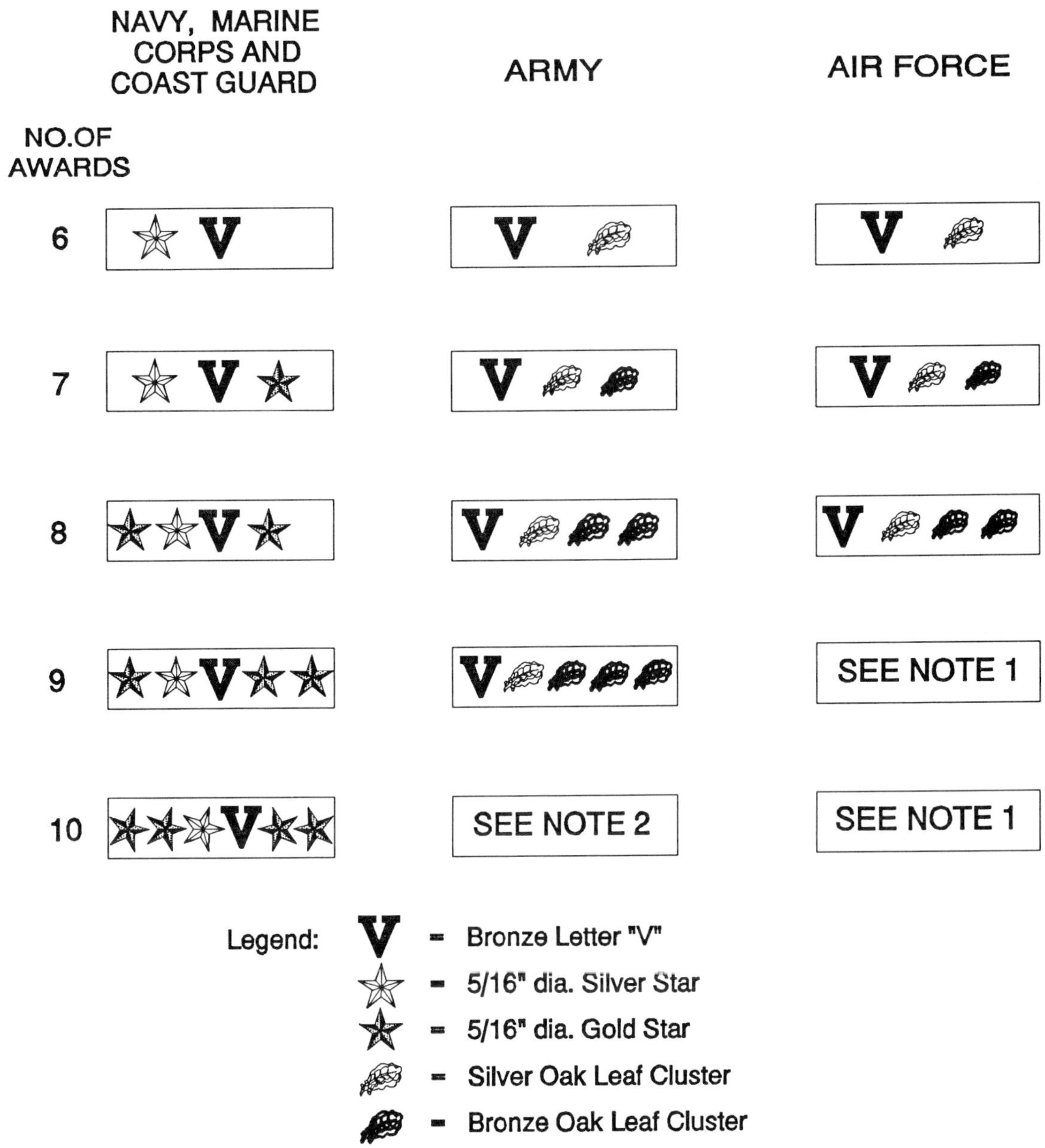

NOTES: 1. Air Force Regulations limit the number of devices which may be worn on a single ribbon to a maximum of four (4). If more than four devices are authorized, a second ribbon is worn containing the excess devices.

2. Army Regulations limit the number of oak leaf clusters which may be worn on a single ribbon to a maximum of four (4).

Plate 20.- PLACEMENT OF THE LETTER "V" WITH OTHER RIBBON DEVICES

Table I- Usage Variations of the Bronze Letter "V"

SERVICE(S)	APPLICABLE MEDALS
Army	Air Medal, Commendation Medal
Navy, Marine Corps	Legion of Merit, Distinguished Flying Cross, Air Medal, Commendation Medal, Achievement Medal (Note: The "V" was no longer awarded with the Legion of Merit and Achievement Medal after the Vietnam War but was reinstituted for awards of the two medals during Operation Desert Storm and thereafter)
Coast Guard	Legion of Merit, Commendation Medal, Achievement Medal
Air Force	Outstanding Unit Award, Organizational Excellence Award

3. The Navy uses the small (3/16") bronze star on its unit awards (i.e., Unit Commendation, Meritorious Unit Commendation and "E" Ribbon) as an additional award device. The Coast Guard, however, uses the large (5/16") gold star on its equivalent unit awards.

4. Until the Department of Defense standardized the practice, most of the Services used a system of bronze numerals to indicate additional awards of the Humanitarian Service Medal. From the outset, however, the Coast Guard utilized small (3/16") bronze and silver stars to denote one and five additional awards of the medal respectively. It is the Coast Guard system that is now in effect for all Branches of the Service (Plate 21).

5. Contrary to other policies covering personal and unit awards, no provisions are made to denote the fifth and subsequent awards of the Navy "E" Ribbon. Upon receipt of the fourth award, the wreathed, silver "E" is worn and no further devices may be affixed to the ribbon after that.

6. Unlike any other Service, the Coast Guard forbids the wear of the oak leaf cluster on its uniform. This requires the substitution of a large (5/16") gold or silver star to denote additional awards of any Joint Service decoration (e.g., DDSM, DSSM, DMSM, JSCM, JSAM) or any award(s) earned while part of the Army or Air Force.

7. The Army permits the wear of devices on the Republic of Vietnam Gallantry Cross Unit Citation (bronze palms plus gold, silver and/or bronze stars) to denote the level of the award as well as subsequent awards. The other Services only allow the display of a single bronze palm.

D. Multiplicity of Device Types

Case D arises from the fact that many different devices can be worn on the same ribbon. Although two might be acceptable, (e.g., letter "V" with gold star, arrowhead with battle star, etc.), things are definitely out of hand when as many as THREE distinct device types can be affixed to the same ribbon. The most extreme examples in the ribbon clutter category are the following:

1. The Navy, which permits the wear of the Presidential Unit Citation with a gold letter "N", a gold globe and a bronze star at the same time.

2. The Coast Guard, which authorizes the simultaneous display of a bronze letter "V", 5/16" gold/silver stars and a silver letter "O" on the ribbons of its Commendation and Achievement Medals.

3. The Navy, which uses a 3/16" bronze star or 5/16" gold and silver stars along with bronze numerals and the bronze letter "V" simultaneously on its version of the Air Medal (see the next section for a more complete discussion of Air Medal device utilization).

NO.OF AWARDS	NAVY, MARINE CORPS AND AIR FORCE	ARMY	COAST GUARD
2	2	1	★
3	3	2	★ ★
4	4	3	★ ★ ★
5	5	4	★ ★ ★ ★
6	6	5	☆

Legend: 1, 2 etc. = Bronze Block Numerals

★ = 3/16" dia. Bronze Star

☆ = 3/16" dia. Silver Star

Plate 21. **ORIGINAL** PLACEMENT OF DEVICES ON THE HUMANITARIAN SERVICE MEDAL (CIRCA 1977 - 1985)

4. Air Medal Devices

Still on the general subject of ribbon appurtenances, we shall now turn our attention to the case of the Air Medal, the classic example of how many different ways the Services can specify the wearing of devices, both now and in the past. As mentioned in the previous section, both the Army and the Navy use the bronze letter "V" on the Air Medal but it is in denoting additional awards that the Services have demonstrated some real Yankee individuality.

Although the Army and Air Force systems (i.e., numerals and oak leaf clusters, respectively) are totally different, they are, at the very least, straightforward and easily understood. It is the Navy, then, that has entered a new dimension by establishing two very distinct categories, strike/flight and individual service, for all awards of the Air Medal, both initial and subsequent.

Strike/flight awards of the Navy Air Medal are indicated by bronze block numerals worn on the right-hand orange stripe (as seen by the viewer). For individual awards, a small (3/16" dia) bronze star is used to indicate the first award while the traditional 5/16" gold stars are used to denote additional individual awards (see Plate 22).

The two different categories have created a situation in which a device is used on a ribbon to denote the INITIAL award of a personal decoration, the first in American medallic history (for purists, it will be noted that the Merchant Marine Gallant Ship Citation Bar is issued with a silver seahorse device and the Navy "E" Ribbon carries a silver letter "E" upon initial issue. Both of these, however, are unit awards rather than decorations).

Just for the record, the Navy had used the above method for many years but discarded it in favor of a system that utilized gold block numerals, placed on the left-hand orange stripe (as seen by the viewer) to denote the total number of individual awards of the Air Medal (see Plate 23).

Both of the above cases were combined with the bronze strike/flight numerals as described above. Use of the gold numerals was not universal, however, and was resisted vigorously by those senior officers who clung tenaciously to their gold stars. So, with the demise of the gold numeral, there is now another body of dissatisfied Navy men. These are the Vietnam-era pilots who earned the medal in great profusion, but now have great difficulty in displaying their true number of awards using 5/16" gold and silver stars.

As for the two other Naval Services, the Marine Corps follows the Navy's lead in using both numerals and 5/16" gold and silver stars. But to close the subject on a final note of confusion, the Coast Guard uses ONLY the 5/16" gold and silver stars to denote additional awards of the Air Medal for all categories of heroic and meritorious achievement in flight. However, strike/flight awards received while serving with Navy units may be worn on the ribbon as prescribed above.

5. Disparate Regulations

As the next chapter in this "Dissertation on Diversity", the following differences in ribbon wear between the various Armed Services are submitted without further comment:

A. The Air Force is the only Branch of the Service to authorize the wear of miniature ribbon bars on the uniform, albeit restricted to the lightweight summer shirt.

B. The Air Force permits a second ribbon to be worn if more than four (4) devices are authorized for wear on a single ribbon bar. The Army also specifies a limit of four (4) oak leaf clusters on the ribbon bar but this leaves the question of a 10th award up in the air since the hypothetical recipient has no way to display the requisite one silver and four bronze oak leaf clusters.

C. Unit awards worn by Army personnel are unique in that the gold frames are physically larger (1/2" vs. 3/8" high) and are worn on the right breast of the Army uniform. This regulation is also applicable to unit awards received from other Services or from foreign governments. If this seems unusual, consider the original Army scheme (circa 1960) that placed the Presidential Unit Citation on the right breast, other U.S. unit awards on the left

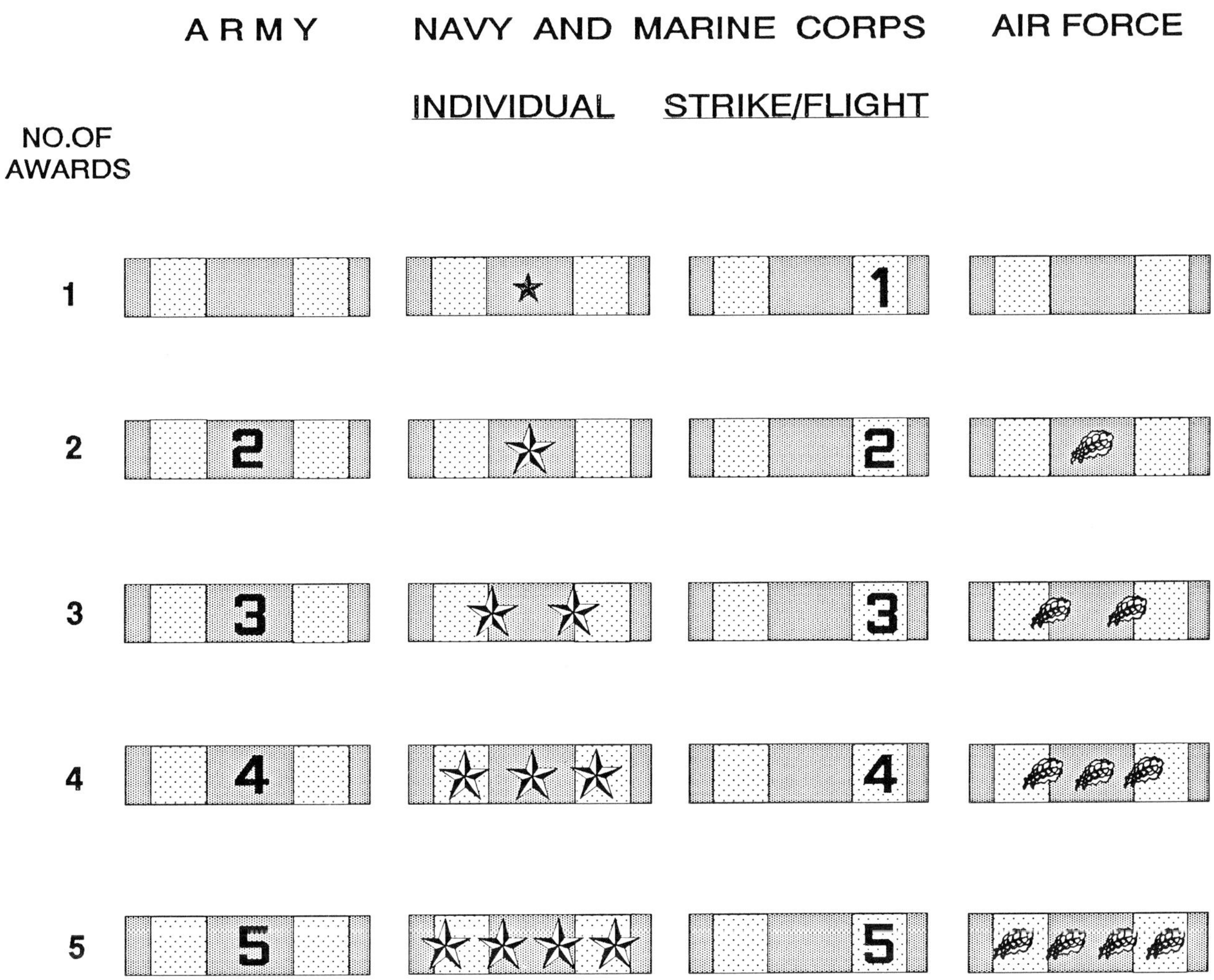

Legend:

= 5/16" dia. Gold Star

= 3/16" dia. Bronze Star

1, 2 etc. = Bronze Block Numerals

= Bronze Oak Leaf Cluster

Plate 22. - PLACEMENT OF DEVICES ON THE AIR MEDAL RIBBON

NAVY AND MARINE CORPS

(INDIVIDUAL AWARDS)

NO.OF AWARDS	(CIRCA 1966-1978)	(CIRCA 1978-1991)
1		
2		
3		
4		
5		

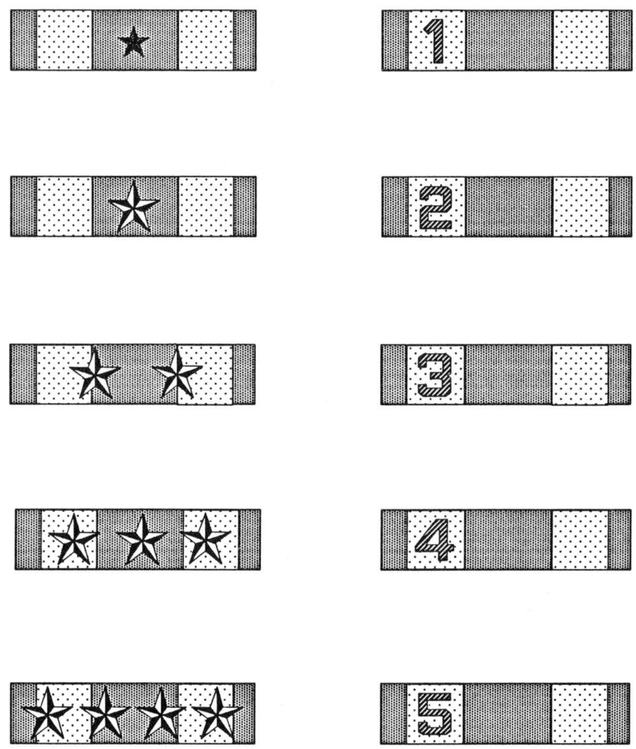

Legend:

☆ = 5/16" dia. Gold Star

★ = 3/16" dia. Bronze Star

1 , 2 etc. = Gold Block Numerals

Plate 23. - **FORMER** NAVY DEVICE USAGE ON THE AIR MEDAL RIBBON

breast amongst the other ribbons, foreign unit citations below all other ribbons on the left breast pocket flap and the Meritorious Unit Commendation in the form of a sew-on patch on the lower right-hand sleeve.

D. The Navy, Marine Corps and Coast Guard follow the "right-side" precedent to a limited extent, requiring ribbons that have no associated medals (e.g., Combat Action, Unit, Marksmanship, etc.) to be worn on the right breast on those occasions when full-sized medals are authorized. But, as before, there is disagreement on the order of wear. The Marine Corps requires a "top to bottom, wearer's right to wearer's left" arrangement while the Navy and Coast Guard specify an "inboard to outboard" display" (see Section 8). By contrast, neither the Army nor the Air Force permits these "ribbon-only" awards to be worn on the uniform when full-size or miniature medals are specified.

E. The Army and the Coast Guard Uniform Regulations stipulate that unit awards with gold frames be worn with the laurel leaves on the frame pointing up. The Marine Corps accomplishes the same goal by requiring the laurel leaves to form a "V" (point down). On the other hand, none of the other awards or uniform regulations mention the subject.

F. The Army is the only Service to permit the wear of unit awards by personnel who did not participate in the action for which it was cited. Any individual joining at a later date may wear the unit award while permanently attached, but must relinquish it upon subsequent reassignment.

G. Army and Marine Corps ribbons may, at the wearer's option, be worn with a 1/8" separation between adjacent rows. The other Services do not permit any such separation.

H. Similarly, the maximum number of ribbons that may be displayed in each row depends on which Service is being discussed. The applicable quotes from the various uniform regulations are offered in Table II without comment:

I. The Marine Corps, in an unfortunate reference to the senior status of the color blue in heraldry, specifies the wear of the ribbon for the Merchant Marine Mariner's Medal in the order of blue, white, red (as seen by an observer) thus putting themselves out of step with all of the other Services as well as the dictates of the awarding agency itself.

J. On a number of occasions, the Services have awarded more than one medal for the same combat action as per Table III.

K. Then consider the refusal of some Services to permit the wear of certain awards of the other Branches. As of this writing, the restrictions existing are shown in Table IV.

L. The Coast Guard, being the hereditary "owners" of the Department of Transportation

Table II - Regulations for Ribbon Wear

SERVICE	REGULATIONS FOR RIBBON WEAR
ARMY:	• No line will contain more than four service ribbons • Unit awards will be worn with not more than three per row
NAVY:	• Worn in horizontal rows of three each
MARINE CORPS	• Normally worn in rows of three, however rows of four may be worn when displaying a large number of awards
COAST GUARD:	• One, two or three ribbons are worn in a single row
AIR FORCE:	• Wear ribbons in multiples of three or four

Table III - Occasions on Which Multiple Awards Were Authorized

DATE	EVENT/ACTION	AWARDS PRESENTED
1937	Attack on Gunboat "Panay" (China)	1. Navy Expeditionary Medal 2. China Service Medal
1941	Defense of Wake Island	1. Asiatic-Pacific Campaign Medal 2. Navy (or Marine Corps) Expeditionary Medal with "Wake Island" clasp 3. Navy Presidential Unit Citation
1941	Defense of the Philippine Islands (U.S. Army personnel)	1. Bronze Star Medal 2. Asiatic-Pacific Campaign Medal 3. Army Presidential Unit Citation 4. Philippine Defense Ribbon (Philippine Government)
1975	Evacuation of Saigon, Republic of Vietnam	1. Armed Forces Expeditionary Medal 2. Humanitarian Service Medal 3. (Some personnel): Combat Action Ribbon plus Navy Unit Commendation or Navy Meritorious Unit Commendation

Table IV - Inter-Service Restrictions on Ribbon Wear

SERVICE	RESTRICTIONS
ARMY	(a) Air Force Longevity Service Award Ribbon (b) Air Force and Navy Marksmanship ribbons (c) Marksmanship Badges awarded by other U.S. Services
MARINE CORPS	(a) Army Combat Medical or Combat Infantryman's Badge must be "traded in" for the Combat Action Ribbon (b) Any award that has no direct Marine Corps equivalent (e.g., Navy Marksmanship Ribbons, Air Force Training and Recognition Ribbons, Army Service Ribbon, etc.)
NAVY	(a) Army badges per the Marine Corps (above) (b) Coast Guard Commandant's Letter of Commendation Ribbon (c) All other awards having no direct Navy equivalent.
COAST GUARD	(a) All training and marksmanship medals/badges/ribbons earned in another branch of the Service. (b) Any award that has no direct Coast Guard equivalent (e.g., Air Force Longevity Service Award Ribbon, Combat Readiness Medal, etc.)
AIR FORCE	(a) No comparable restrictions instituted.

(originally the Treasury Department) Gold and Silver Life Saving Medals, treats these awards as military decorations. As can be seen in the Coast Guard ribbon chest (Plate 13) they are afforded a specific position in the Coast Guard order of precedence. All other Services, however, consider them to be non-military decorations with no absolute precedence within the group.

M. As another sidelight to this discussion, the Coast Guard is alone in specifying an additional award device (the large 5/16" gold star) for the Life Saving Medals.

N. Coast Guard is also the only Service to include awards to civilians in its list of military decorations. The cases in point are the three Department of Transportation awards listed in Plate 13 which may be worn as shown on the uniform.

O. Finally, the ultimate in awards with little significance is the Army Service Ribbon. Since this ribbon is awarded to all officers or enlisted men who have successfully completed <u>any</u> entry-level training course, EVERY PERSON in the U.S. Army is entitled to wear it. Unlike a true general service award (e.g., National Defense Service Medal), the Army Service Ribbon has no termination date and requires no "service" of any kind.

6. Strange Common Regulations

Thus far, this article has dealt only with the differences between the various U.S. awards regulations. As a final chapter, it would have been refreshing to report that the remaining areas, in which the Services all agree amongst themselves, made absolute sense from the standpoints of logic and tradition. Unfortunately, this is not the case as can be seen in the following examples:

A. The medals associated with the Philippine Defense, Liberation and Independence Ribbons, although issued and sanctioned for wear by a friendly foreign government, may <u>not</u> be worn on the U.S. military uniform. All of the applicable Uniform Regulations refer to these awards as "Ribbons" rather than "Medals" and permit only the ribbon to be worn.

B. Ribbon devices, in most cases, are worn to denote the award of clasps to certain service medals (e.g., World War I Victory Medal, American Defense Service Medal, Navy Expeditionary Medal, etc.). The sole exception to the rule is the World War II Occupation Medal, which makes no provisions for a device in cases where both clasps have been awarded.

C. The distinctive ribbons associated with certain United Nations medals may not be worn on the U.S. military uniform. Army or Air Force personnel who took part in the Western New Guinea (UNTEA) or India/Pakistan (UNMOGIP) operations must wear the "standard" U.N. Observer ribbon normally associated with the UNTSO and UNOGIL medals (light blue with a single white stripe near each edge).

D. A second award of the Philippine Presidential Unit Citation (for service during disaster relief operations in 1972) is denoted by a small bronze star on the ribbon. However, a similar second award of the Republic of Korea Presidential Unit Citation for the <u>same</u> operation goes unrecognized.

E. Finally, consider the case of the "Wintered Over" clasps and disks used on the Antarctica Service Medal. In a classic example of reverse logic, the time-honored sequence of bronze, silver and gold was altered to bronze-gold-silver to denote 1, 2, and 3 winters respectively.

12. NOTES AND COMMENTS

As indicated in the Introduction to this book, certain errors/omissions have been noted by the authors subsequent to the preparation of the color plates. In addition, there are certain areas of text which require further clarification where space was at a premium. These will be referenced to the applicable page(s).

Page 19: The Coast Guard's latest (and most senior) award, the Transportation Distinguished Service Medal, was approved too late for inclusion in this book. It takes precedence over the Coast Guard Distinguished Service Medal and is awarded "...by the Secretary of Transportation to a member of the Coast Guard who has provided exceptionally meritorious service in a duty of great responsibility while assigned to the Department of Transportation...". It has already been named the "Commandant's Medal" since its award is expected to be limited to the most senior echelons of the Coast Guard. With a projection of only one award per year, it may already rank with some of the rarest awards in the world.

Page 21, Items 20 and 26: Lifesaving medals are awarded to military personnel only if the individual is on a leave or liberty status. Otherwise, a military decoration is more appropriate.

Page 21, Item 21: The Bronze Star Medal for meritorious service was authorized for those awarded either the Combat Infantryman Badge or Combat Medical Badge between 7 December 1941 and 2 September 1945. Since the two badges were not awarded until July, 1943, those Army infantrymen and medics whose meritorious achievements in combat prior to July, 1943 are confirmable in writing may still be eligible for the Bronze Star.

Page 23, Item 29: The Army Commendation Medal, originally a ribbon only, is authorized for award to any Army member who received a letter or certificate of commendation signed by a Major General or higher for meritorious achievement between 7 December 1941 and 1 January 1946.

Page 23, Item 30: The Navy Commendation Medal is authorized for award to any member of the U.S. Navy, Marine Corps or Coast Guard who has received a letter of commendation from the Secretary of the Navy, the Commander in Chief of the Pacific or Atlantic Fleet or Commander of the Fleet Marine Force, Pacific for an act of heroism or meritorious service performed between 6 December 1941 and 11 January 1944. Subsequent to the above period, personnel may apply for the medal if they possess a letter of commendation from the same higher authority providing the award is specifically mentioned.

Page 25, Items 47-51: Using the traditional sequence of "Senior Service First", these items should be listed in the order: 48, 49, 51, 50 and 47

Page 27, Items 66 and 67: The award criteria for the two Occupation Medals are worth repeating since they rank highest on the list of items which many veterans forget to claim. The guidelines are the same for both, requiring a member of the Army, Navy, Marine Corps or Coast Guard to have served 30 consecutive days in any of the occupied territories after VE-Day and/or VJ-Day.

Page 30, Items 90a, 91a: The devices should be placed on the respective ribbons as follows:

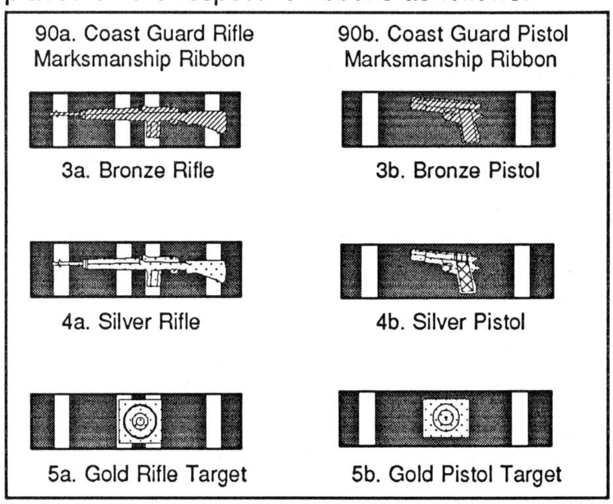

Page 33, Item 96: Some confusion seems to exist on the criteria for the Philippine Independence Ribbon/Medal. The original standard ("...present for duty in the Philippines on 4 July 1946...") was modified in 1953 and, since that time, sentiment (and some very competent authorities) seem to favor the award to U.S. personnel who won either the Philippine Defense or Philippine Liberation Ribbons. However, U.S. military regulations require the receipt of **both** the Defense and Liberation Ribbons.

REQUEST PERTAINING TO MILITARY RECORDS

Please read instructions on the reverse. If more space is needed, use plain paper.

PRIVACY ACT OF 1974 COMPLIANCE INFORMATION. The following information is provided in accordance with 5 U.S.C. 552a(e)(3) and applies to this form. Authority for collection of the information is 44 U.S.C. 2907, 3101, and 3103, and E.O. 9397 of November 22, 1943. Disclosure of the information is voluntary. The principal purpose of the information is to assist the facility servicing the records in locating and verifying the correctness of the requested records or information to answer your inquiry. Routine uses of the information as established and published in accordance with 5 U.S.C.a(e)(4)(D) include the transfer of relevant information to appropriate Federal, State, local, or foreign agencies for use in civil, criminal, or regulatory investigations or prosecution. In addition, this form will be filed with the appropriate military records and may be transferred along with the record to another agency in accordance with the routine uses established by the agency which maintains the record. If the requested information is not provided, it may not be possible to service your inquiry.

SECTION I—INFORMATION NEEDED TO LOCATE RECORDS (Furnish as much as possible)

1. NAME USED DURING SERVICE *(Last, first, and middle)*	2. SOCIAL SECURITY NO.	3. DATE OF BIRTH	4. PLACE OF BIRTH

5. ACTIVE SERVICE, PAST AND PRESENT (For an effective records search, it is important that ALL service be shown below)

BRANCH OF SERVICE *(Also, show last organization, if known)*	DATES OF ACTIVE SERVICE		*Check one*		SERVICE NUMBER DURING THIS PERIOD
	DATE ENTERED	DATE RELEASED	OFFI-CER	EN-LISTED	

6. RESERVE SERVICE, PAST OR PRESENT *If "none," check here* ▶ ☐

a. BRANCH OF SERVICE	b. DATES OF MEMBERSHIP		c. *Check one*		d. SERVICE NUMBER DURING THIS PERIOD
	FROM	TO	OFFI-CER ☐	EN-LISTED ☐	

7. NATIONAL GUARD MEMBERSHIP *(Check one):* ☐ a. ARMY ☐ b. AIR FORCE ☐ c. NONE

d. STATE	e. ORGANIZATION	f. DATES OF MEMBERSHIP		g. *Check one*		h. SERVICE NUMBER DURING THIS PERIOD
		FROM	TO	OFFI-CER ☐	EN-LISTED ☐	

8. IS SERVICE PERSON DECEASED ☐ YES ☐ NO *If "yes," enter date of death.*

9. IS (WAS) INDIVIDUAL A MILITARY RETIREE OR FLEET RESERVIST ☐ YES ☐ NO

SECTION II—REQUEST

1. EXPLAIN WHAT INFORMATION OR DOCUMENTS YOU NEED; OR, CHECK ITEM 2; OR, COMPLETE ITEM 3

2. IF YOU ONLY NEED A STATEMENT OF SERVICE *check here* ☐

3. *LOST SEPARATION DOCUMENT REPLACEMENT REQUEST (Complete a or b, and c.)*			
☐	a. REPORT OF SEPARATION *(DD Form 214 or equivalent)*	YEAR ISSUED	*This contains information normally needed to determine eligibility for benefits. It may be furnished only to the veteran, the surviving next of kin, or to a representative with veteran's signed release (item 5 of this form).*
☐	b. DISCHARGE CERTIFICATE	YEAR ISSUED	*This shows only the date and character at discharge. It is of little value in determining eligibility for benefits. It may be issued only to veterans discharged honorably or under honorable conditions; or, if deceased, to the surviving spouse.*
	c. EXPLAIN HOW SEPARATION DOCUMENT WAS LOST		

4. EXPLAIN PURPOSE FOR WHICH INFORMATION OR DOCUMENTS ARE NEEDED

6. REQUESTER

a. IDENTIFICATION *(check appropriate box)*

☐ Same person identified in Section I ☐ Surviving spouse

☐ Next of kin (relationship) __________

☐ Other (specify)

b. SIGNATURE *(see instruction 3 on reverse side)* DATE OF REQUEST

5. RELEASE AUTHORIZATION, IF REQUIRED *(Read instruction 3 on reverse side)*

I hereby authorize release of the requested information/documents to the person indicated at right (item 7).

VETERAN SIGN HERE ▶ __________

(If signed by other than veteran show relationship to veteran.)

7. *Please type or print clearly* — COMPLETE RETURN ADDRESS

Name, number and street, city, State and ZIP code

TELEPHONE NO. *(include area code)* ▶

180-106 NSN 7540-00-142-9360 **STANDARD FORM 180 (Rev. 7-86)** Prescribed by NARA (36 CFR 1228.162(a))

14. BIBLIOGRAPHY

Abbott, P.E. and Tamplin, J.M.A.- *British Gallantry Awards*, 1971
Adjutant General of the Army- *American Decorations 1862-1926*, 1927
Belden, B.L.- *United States War Medals*, 1916
Committee on Veterans' Affairs, U.S. Senate- *Medal of Honor Recipients 1863-1978*, 1979
Dept. of Defense Manual DOD 1348.33M- *Manual of Military Decorations & Awards*, 1990
Dorling, H.T.- *Ribbons and Medals*, 1983
Gleim, A.F.- *United States Medals of Honor 1862-1989*, 1989
Gleim, A.F.- *War Department Gallantry Citations for Pre W W I Service*, 1986
Inter-American Defense Board- *Norms for Protocol, Symbols, Insignia and Gifts*, 1984
Kerrigan, E.- *American Badges and Insignia*, 1967
Kerrigan, E.- *American Medals and Decorations*, 1990
Kerrigan, E.- *American War Medals and Decorations*, 1971
McDowell, C.P.- *Military and Naval Decorations of the United States*, 1984
National Geographic Magazine, December, 1919
National Geographic Society- *Insignia and Decorations of the U.S. Armed Forces*, 1944
U.S. Air Force Manual 900-3- *Dress and Personal Appearance of U.S.A.F. Personnel*, 1989
U.S. Air Force Regulation 900-48- *Individual and Unit Awards and Decorations*, 1989
U.S. Army Regulation 670-1- *Wear and Appearance of Army Uniforms and Insignia*, 1992
U.S. Army Regulation 672-5-1- *Military Awards*, 1989
U.S. Coast Guard Instruction M1020.6A- *U.S. Coast Guard Uniform Regulations*, 1985
U.S. Coast Guard Instruction M1650.25A- *Medals and Awards Manual*, 1992
U.S. Marine Corps Order P1020.34- *U.S. Marine Corps Uniform Regulations*, 1988
U.S. Navy Instruction SECNAVINST 1650.1F- *Navy and Marine Corps Awards Manual*, 1991
U.S. Navy Instruction SECNAVINST 15665G- *United States Navy Uniform Regulations*, 1987
U.S. Navy Manual NAVPERS 15,790- *Decorations, Medals, Ribbons and Badges of the United States Navy, Marine Corps and Coast Guard, 1861-1948*, 1 July 1950
Vietnam Council on Foreign Relations- *Awards & Decorations of Vietnam*, 1972
Wilkins, P.A.- *The History of the Victoria Cross*, 1904
Wyllie, Col. R.E.- *Orders, Decorations and Insignia*, 1921

---

15. INDEX

NOTE: Numbers in Bold Italics Denote Illustrations